• What People Are Saying

"This book brings together practical experience and common sense to provide essential financial skills to make prudent decisions in life, especially important for Californians preparing to enter into a career, start a family or buy a home." —California State Assemblywoman Cathleen Galgiani

"This course is one step in the right direction ..."

—Jeff Davi, Real Estate Commissioner, California Department of Real Estate

"This textbook is a great primer to introduce students to the basics of personal finances."

—Christopher Thornberg, PhD, Principal, Beacon Economics, Los Angeles

"The White Picket Fence series will undoubtedly offer a solid foundation to support Californians in making informed and sustainable financial decisions."

—Jacqueline Carlisle, Executive Director NID-Housing Counseling Agency (A HUD National Intermediary), Oakland

"Students and educators alike will benefit from the 4 "Bs" in these 'affordable housing' times."

—Mary Ellen Brady, President, California Community College Real Estate Educators' Association and Real Estate Department Chair, Cerritos College, Norwalk

"Finally, real estate information in an understandable format that every person from 9th grade through retirement should know about owning real property."

—Dr. D. Grogan, Professor of Real Estate, GRI, CRS, CPM, El Camino College, Torrance

"I fully endorse, applaud this effort, and wish it had been around back in 2004."

—Paul Rozo, CEO, Paramount Residential Mortgage Group, Corona

"This content can help the average buyer graduate into a sophisticated homeowner."

—Michael Silver, Financial Services Advisor, QTK, Inc., North Lake Tahoe

"Forget hairspray, helmets, and handguns, this is the information you need to protect yourself in the 21st century!"

—Dan Piraro, *Bizarro*, cartoonist

Financial Sense to White Picket Fence

- Other Instructor and Student Study Guides
  are available from the California Community College Real Estate Education Center.

- **Real Estate Finance**

- **Real Estate Economics**

- **Real Estate Law**

- **Real Estate Principles**

- **Real Estate Practice**

- **Escrow**

- **Appraisal**

- **Mortgage Brokering and Lending**

- **Common Interest Developments**

- **Property Management**

Financial Sense to White Picket Fence

Budgeting • Borrowing • Buying • Beyond

by Chris Sorensen

Executive Director
Homeownership Education Learning Program (H.E.L.P.)™

California Community Colleges
Real Estate Education Center

Published by
The California Community College Real Estate Education Center
City College of San Francisco

California Community Colleges
Real Estate Education Center

This project was completed by the Real Estate Education Center, housed at the City College of San Francisco, under the direction of the Community Colleges Chancellor's Office. This book is a derivative of a contractual agreement with the California Department of Real Estate and is not itself a product of that agreement. It is the policy of the Real Estate Education Center not to discriminate against any person on the basis of race, color, national origin, sex, or disability in all of its educational and employment programs and activities.

First Printing: 2011

ISBN: 978-0-692-01326-7

Sample forms reprinted with permission of the California Association of REALTORS®, endorsement not implied.

Clip Art, Media Gallery, and Excel Templates used with permission of Microsoft®, all rights reserved.

Images in the Ask the Expert boxes are from *Bizarro*, used by permission of Dan Piraro, all rights reserved.

Cover and interior design and composition by Leigh McLellan Design.

Disclaimer: The views and opinions expressed in this guide are those of the author, editor, instructor, lecturer, or course sponsor. They do not constitute an endorsement by the California Department of Real Estate or the California Community Colleges Chancellor's Office. Examples of analysis performed within this guide and material are only examples. Assumptions made within the analysis are not reflective of the position of any State of California entity. No grant funds were used in the creation of this guide. The copyright was transferred to the California Community Colleges Chancellor's Office by the author and the guide is distributed by the California Community Colleges Real Estate Education Center.

For inquiries, please contact:
The California Community College Real Estate Education Center
City College of San Francisco—Downtown Campus
88 Fourth Street, Room 324
San Francisco, CA 94103

Web site: www.CCSF.edu/Real_Estate_Education_Center

Dedication

To my father for always being a living example to follow.

To my beautiful bride, Shellie, you truly motivate me to be a man of faith, love, and passion.

Finally, to my boys, may you be blessed by giving first and asking questions second.

Letter from the Commissioner of Real Estate

STATE OF CALIFORNIA — BUSINESS, TRANSPORTATION AND HOUSING AGENCY   EDMUND G. BROWN JR., *Governor*

DEPARTMENT OF REAL ESTATE *Serving Californians Since 1917*
OFFICE OF THE COMMISSIONER
2201 Broadway
P.O. Box 187000
Sacramento, CA 95818
(916) 227-0782

March 25, 2011

Dear Fellow Californians:

I am very pleased you have selected "Financial Sense to White Picket Fence," a financial literacy course. The original live seminars, webinars, and instructor guide were created through a partnership of the California Community Colleges Real Estate Education Center and the Department of Real Estate's Financial Literacy Task Force. This companion book provides a primer for Californians contemplating the rent verses own financial decision.

This guide was designed to help California consumers prepare for home ownership. It was created by its original course instructor, an experienced real estate broker and lender, Mr. Chris Sorenson, President of the Homeowner Education Learning Program (H.E.L.P). The home buying process begins well before one starts to tour properties. The Department of Real Estate encourages ALL Californians, from young adults through senior citizens, to embrace the power of real estate. With this knowledge, consumers will gain greater understanding in their real estate transactions and financing, but just as importantly, consumers will be less likely to be victimized by real estate fraud.

The last few years have taught us many lessons about the importance of financing as it relates to the purchase of real property. The decisions we make relating to a home loan or one's personal finances can have significant long-term impact on our lives. I do not want to see another generation of Californians go through the same experience we have recently gone through with the mortgage meltdown. This guide is yet another step in the right direction to ensure that future homebuyers are better educated and more prepared for their purchase or refinance. Consider contacting your local California Community College to enroll in a financial literacy or consumer protection course. It is my hope that a similar course becomes a requirement of California's K–12 curriculum.

If our department can provide you with any further assistance, I encourage you to contact our Financial Literacy Chairperson, Dionne Faulk, Managing Deputy Commissioner, at (213) 620-2555 or via email at Dionne Faulk@dre.ca.gov.

Good luck and thank you for helping to improve our great State!

Sincerely,

Real Estate Commissioner

California Financial Literacy Live Seminars

San Joaquin Delta College, Stockton, June 19, 2010

Riverside City College, Riverside, September 25, 2010

El Camino College, Torrance, October 16, 2010

San Jose City College, San Jose, November 6, 2010

Acknowledgements

This Financial Literacy guide is published by the California Community Colleges Real Education Center under the guidance of the California Community College Chancellor's Office. It is intended as a companion text to the popular "Financial Sense to White Picket Fence" live seminar offered by your local community college. The guide also functions as a stand-alone primer for all Californians seeking assistance in the rent verses homeownership decision.

Understanding of real estate financial transactions is critical to all Californians. This guide is for you whether you are purchasing your first home, renting, or refinancing an existing mortgage. California recently experienced a challenging financial impact caused in part by the lack of consumer knowledge. It is the goal of this guide to introduce and foster an appreciation of the financial commitment required for homeownership. With the power of real estate knowledge, consumers will not only have greater understanding of their real estate transactions and financing, but will be less likely to be victims of real estate fraud.

This guide was adapted from live seminars offered in 2010 at four California Community Colleges: San Joaquin Delta College in Stockton, Riverside City College in Riverside, El Camino College in Torrance, and San Jose City College in San Jose. The content and lecture material from these seminars was developed further into a series of four weekly webinars. Finally, the live streaming video and archived video were filmed and developed by 3C Media Solutions, the educational media distribution network dedicated to assisting the California Community Colleges. Content and website information derived from these seminars was supplemented and published at: http://www.CaliforniaFinancialLiteracy.org. This Financial Literacy guide is the product of these efforts.

The author and the publisher extend their gratitude to the many educational, professional, and industry organizations, as well as consumers, who are committed to homeownership and stable communities. Their involvement in the live seminars, webinars, streaming live video, and creation of an instructor guide and this companion guide is inspiring. Through and with them, we are confident that Californians are poised to become sustainable homeowners creating more stable communities.

The following are many of those involved in the success of the live seminars held at community colleges throughout California in 2010. Special thanks to California Community Colleges for hosting the Financial Literacy seminars, and for your flexibility and hospitality.

- California Department of Real Estate
  - Jeff Davi, Real Estate Commissioner, California Department of Real Estate
  - Barbara Bigby, Chief Deputy Commissioner, California Department of Real Estate
  - Dionne Young Faulk, Managing Deputy Commissioner, Financial Literacy Outreach Program Chairperson
  - California Department of Real Estate Financial Literacy Outreach Task Force
  - Tom Pool, Assistant Commissioner, Legislation and Public Information
  - Sandra Knau, Managing Deputy Commissioner, Licensing Section
  - Shelly Harkins, Managing Deputy Commissioner, Education, Research and Examinations
  - Rosa Arellano, Abegail Buslon, Angela Cash, Anotonio Chavez, Veronica Corpin, Angela Guevara, Luke Martin, Irene Reyes, Apollo Ubani, Anthony Vo, and Kimberly Wessler, California Department of Real Estate, Los Angeles and Sacramento Offices

- Chancellor's Office, California Community College
  - Dr. Jack Scott, Chancellor
  - W. Charles Wisely, EdD, Specialist
  - California Community College Real Estate Endowment and Advisory Board

- California State Department of Financial Institutions
  - Mathew Velasquez, Outreach Coordinator
  - Lezlie Cannon, Public Information Office Analyst

- San Joaquin Delta College
  - Vince Brown, Vice President
  - Hazel Hill, Vice President
  - Ron Wiley, Real Estate Program Chair
  - Janet Truscott, Instructor, Business Division
  - Claudia Mackey, Coordinator, Community Education
  - Jim Vergara, Public Information Officer
  - Ann Cammack, Food Services
  - Cathleen Galgiani, California State Assembly Member—Tracy District 17
  - Ann Johnson, Mayor of Stockton
  - Ken Vogel, San Joaquin County Supervisor—Lodi District 4

- Riverside Community College
  - Dr. Tom Harris, PhD, Acting President
  - Kristen Van Hala, Administrative Assistant, President's Office
  - Diana Meza, Community Relations Specialist
  - Cheryl Ruzak, Food Services
  - Rod Pacheco, District Attorney, County of Riverside
  - Andy Melendrez, City Council Member, Ward 2, City of Riverside

- El Camino Community College
  - Dr. Thomas Fallo, PhD, President
  - Dean Jose Anaya, Community Advancement Division

- Donna Grogan, Real Estate Program Chair
- Karen Latuner-Hess, Tech Prep Coordinator, Career & Technical Education Programs
- Orasa Chantravutikorn, Food service

- San Jose Community College
  - Douglas M. Treadway, PhD, Acting President
  - Kishan Vujjeni, Department Chair, Business & Services Careers
  - John Black, Real Estate Program Chair
  - Linda Jimenez, Business Services

- City College of San Francisco
  - Dr. Don Q. Griffin, Chancellor
  - Albert Dixon, Director, Small Business Development Center
  - David Dore, Business Department Chair
  - Robin Pugh, Small Business Institute Coordinator, Instructional Support
  - Leonel "Leo" Bello, Real Estate Program Chair, Spanish Translation and Subtitles
  - Pauline Hee, Grant Accounting
  - Craig Easley, Staff, Real Estate Education Center

- Production
  - Program management: Christine Chappell, Homeownership Education Learning Program (H.E.L.P.)™
  - Volunteer extraordinaire: Ivan Navarro, Broker, National Association of Hispanic Real Estate Professionals (NAHREP)
  - Logistics: Presidio Technical and Administrative Services
  - Videography: Grouchy Tiger Productions
  - Photography: Kim Romena, Margaret Light, Richard Whitehead
  - Streaming video: 3C Media Solutions, Palomar College
  - Transcription services: Automatic Sync Technologies
  - Editing services: Marcy Protteau
  - Design and composition: Leigh McLellan Design

- Gift accommodations: Bodega Bay Lodge & Spa and Monterey Plaza Hotel & Spa

There are additional individuals who graciously provided their support with news coverage, printing and distributing fliers, organizing student groups, shuttling staff on last-minute errands, and staffing vendor tables for community outreach. This was a labor of commitment to Californians in the interest of their financial well-being. Many thanks to all unsung Financial Literacy friends for your assistance and support.

Sincerely,

Carol Jensen

Carol A. Jensen, Director,
California Community College Real Estate Education Center

Contents

Preface

We live in a world where the ability to borrow is essential. Credit has been relatively easy to obtain in California for the past decade. As many individuals can attest, credit is sometimes extended even without apparent ability to repay the debt. Many lenders even seem to encourage us to take on far more debt than we could possibly handle. But management of personal and real estate debt is often ignored until the borrower is in a crisis.

To prevent prospective homeowners from facing this crisis, the California Department of Real Estate is collaborating with the California Community College Chancellor's Office to encourage financial literacy throughout California. The California Community College Real Estate Education Center created this companion guide to reach out to an even larger audience than was possible with our live seminars. We named these live seminars "Financial Sense to White Picket Fence" and held them at four California community colleges in 2010. If "Financial Sense to White Picket Fence" can express to you, the reader, that you have the right, ability, and responsibility and to take full control of your financial future, we have achieved our goal. Thank you community college instructors and community education program directors throughout California for bringing this seminar to your campuses during 2011 and making this effort part of your future curriculum.

A team of dedicated people who collectively have decades of aggregate personal experience as presidents of mortgage lending firms, real estate practitioners, small business academics, and a former mayor developed the live seminars, webinar, and this guide. High school students considering credit card use to seniors contemplating reverse mortgages can benefit from the following pages. I hope that the information will help you avoid the mistakes that have devastated the finances of so many Californians.

This guide is by no means comprehensive of all the information that you will need to buy a home. I do hope it will introduce you to practical financial topics and inspire you to seek additional information from all of the additional resources at your disposal. Financial literacy can make the difference between barely surviving from month to month or realizing many of your financial goals and dreams. The more you learn and put this powerful knowledge to use, the brighter your financial future will be.

Warmest regards,

Chris Sorensen

How to Use These Materials

The author suggests using this guide in several learning methods.

1. As a companion guide for student use during a live *Financial Sense to White Picket Fence* seminar offered by a California community college.

2. As a companion guide for student use while viewing *Financial Sense to White Picket Fence* pre-recorded webinar modules. Prerecorded webinars entitled *Budgeting, Borrowing, Buying* and *Beyond* are accessible free of charge at our website: http://www.CaliforniaFinancialLiteracy.org

3. As a stand-alone primer for individual study of financial literacy concepts. Augment your study with exercises, references, websites, and further reading found at our website: http://www.CaliforniaFinancialLiteracy.org

Test yourself and validate your learning as you work through the modules. Each module has specific learning objectives. The exhibits summarize key learning points that help focus your learning. Handouts and exercises are provided to reinforce your study with hands-on exercises. The Multiple Choice Quiz is provided at the conclusion of the guide to test your subject mastery. Answers are provided later in the text. Finally, the Self-Assessment Rubric allows you to assess your progress relative to your initial financial literacy self-assessment. The sample Certificate of Participation is awarded to individuals enrolling in a live community college offered seminar.

Your evaluation and critique of live seminars and this companion guide are encouraged. Feel free to complete the Course Evaluation and /or contact the program directly via email at Information@CaliforniaFinancialLiteracy.org

If you seek additional financial literacy or consumer protection classes, please contact your local California community college. Alternatively, please see a listing of live seminars scheduled in your community posted on the website.

Introduction

Is financial literacy important? Financial "ill-literacy" is the reason many find themselves in crisis today. Many people of all income levels have lost their homes or are in the process of losing them. Until you are in this situation, you may not really appreciate how important financial literacy has become. Lenders may say you qualify for a property during the home loan application process, but do you really qualify? Does qualification by the lender's standards mean that you can actually afford the home and all the expenses that go along with it? Historically, lenders have qualified people at or just above their financial means. In doing so, borrowers are often placed, statistically speaking, just one paycheck away from financial disaster.

This course will endeavor to teach you that it is OK to say "no" to financial over-extension. Once you develop your own personal budget, understand your individual lifestyle, and understand your priorities, you will see that it is OK to tell the lender, "Thank you, but no thank you." A $200,000 home may make more sense for you than the $250,000 home for which they may have qualified you." You—not the lenders—are looking after your financial best interests. This course will give you the knowledge to confidently assess your situation and make sustainable homeownership choices.

One of the goals of this course is to ensure you understand the need to look beyond the goal of obtaining a home; it is critically important to focus on retaining it. For the greatest chance of success, homebuyers need to recognize this before they begin to shop for a home. For 90% of Americans, a residential home purchase is the largest investment they will ever make. Beyond that, it is also one of the most emotional investments. Home is the place where you see your daughter walk down the stairs in her prom dress; where your five-year-old is overwhelmed with excitement over the new red bike under the Christmas tree. Home is where you sit and relax in the morning reading the Sunday paper. Our connection to home is often deeply emotional, making the loss of a home that much more traumatic than the loss of other investments.

Currently, two-thirds of all Americans live month-to-month, one paycheck away from financial ruin. Less than ten percent of high school graduates receive any type of financial education in school. How many of us learned to read the *Wall Street Journal* or to balance a checkbook in school? These skills are invaluable. Only one-third of America's baby boom generation, the greatest consumption generation ever, has saved enough money for retirement. Many people are just beginning to rebuild their financial security right before their original planned retirement. This is devastating to our society. We can do better by re-educating children and ourselves, by enrolling in courses such as this one, that teach us the skills we need to ensure financial stability. If we spread the message of financial literacy, we can help set the next generation up for greater success.

The cost of financial illiteracy is high. Imagine that you have been in your home for 25 years. A lender assured you five years ago that you qualify for a home equity line of credit secured by your principal residence. You subsequently lose your job, cannot make the mortgage payments, and are now in foreclosure. The money is borrowed; therefore, it must be paid back. You suddenly realize that after 25 years, your family must vacate the property and live somewhere else. This is heartbreaking. You are in tears because you must explain to your nine-year-old daughter and ten-year-old son that they must say good-bye to their neighborhood friends. The children cry and are upset with you because the family must leave their home. In addition to financial disaster, the family is now dealing with a disruption of schools and neighborhood, the children's sense of stability is undermined, and the parents feel like failures. This scenario has played out across America millions of times in the past few years. Shockingly, 50% of the people who lose their homes do not make a single phone call to learn of their options. Why? People are extremely stressed, confused and simply do not know what to do or where to get help.

Many Californians are not feeling very stable right now with respect to their homeownership. Many of you know people who are struggling or have already lost their homes. These are not just statistics, these are people we work with, friends and family; the stories are personal. This is the reason we are so passionate about financial literacy. Individuals reading this guide or engaged in the classroom are the next generation of homebuyers. Even if you are a homeowner right now, this course is relevant to you because we need to—and must—do better than we have done in the past. We have millions of homeowners and prospective homeowners focused on buying a home for shelter rather than thinking of homeownership as a financial investment. We want to create financial stability for sustainable homeownership, stable communities, and a better, stronger California. Welcome to "Financial Sense to White Picket Fence."

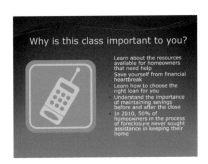

In this class, we will cover four major areas: Budgeting, Borrowing, Buying, and Beyond. Because laying the proper foundation is so important for later success, we begin with an in-depth look at budgeting and tracking expenses. We then proceed to the borrowing process and the steps involved in getting a real estate loan. After that, the fun part begins, and we will discuss buying your first home and going through escrow. Historically, most of the problems in closing the deal for a home purchase unveil themselves right before the close of escrow. This is often the fault of the originating loan officer or real estate professional. It can also result from information uncovered at the last minute. The last topic is perhaps the most important—what happens beyond the close of the deal? Here we explore what you need to do to make sure you keep the home for which you worked so hard.

Module 1: Budgeting

• What is a Budget?

What is a budget and why must it be so detailed? A budget is a plan that outlines an individual's or family's financial goals. While the idea of a budget is simple, the reality is far from it. Most of us do not budget. National statistics indicate that more than 97% of Americans do not pay a single penny more than the minimum payment required by the lender towards their mortgage. Why? We often buy up to or above our financial means. Do you have money left in your checking account on the 29th of the month? It is time for us to change our behavior, and to plan our budgets so that we pay down debt sooner rather than later.

• Action Plan

Think of a budget as an action plan, instead of a hard-to-achieve, limiting set of rules. None of us (except a very, very few) can afford everything we want. Spending always involves a choice. Using a budget means that you keep your eye on the big picture so that you can attain your larger financial goals. It helps you make the choices today that are going to move you forward. It helps you to allocate resources and formulate a plan that works.

A successful budget is not a laundry list of how you would like to spend your money. It needs to start with your current spending patterns. You cannot create a budget that you will be able to follow if you do not pay attention to how you are spending your money every day. For a budget to be successful, you must frequently review it and add or delete expenses accordingly. For example, if you discover that it just is not possible to reduce your food spending after two months of budgeting a certain amount, it is time to change or adjust the budget to something you can successfully meet.

In the western United States, the average household income was $68,031 for 2009, before taxes. How do we spend that money?

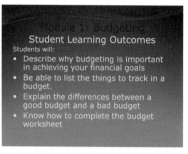

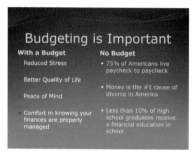

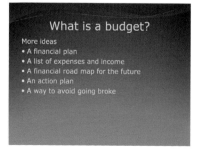

❓ Ask the Expert

Question: How should somebody who is self-employed budget?

Answer: Budgeting for the self-employed is a challenge because income is often sporadic. They may have one great month and then go another three to five weeks before they get another paycheck. The best thing to do is to save aggressively when you do have income, to help cover against those times that income is down. This advice is also relevant to individuals who are not self-employed, but have irregular income for other reasons.

Therefore, if you are self-employed and receive a $10,000 commission check, you have not "profited" by $10,000. You have overhead, research

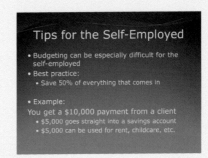

and development expenses, marketing expenses and many other expenses that are on going to run your business. Most Fortune 500 companies are happy to count 15% of their gross earnings as net profit. The rest goes back into the business. If you are self-employed, you should try to do the same. The least you should do if you work on commission sales is take 50% of your check and set it aside.

Typically, housing costs are about 35% of our earnings and car expenditures are about 15%. Entertainment expenses are between 5% and 6% of earnings.[1]

• What is Your Budget Window?

Budget projections are extremely important because they give you a working goal. When budgeting, consider the next three to five years. Your monthly and semi-annual budgets are "mini goals" That help you work toward your long-term future goals. It is important to check periodically on your mini-goal status, but you need to be focused on the future. It is great to have a plan for 30 to 50 years down the road. Looking far ahead has tremendous rewards. Long-term does not have to be 30 years,

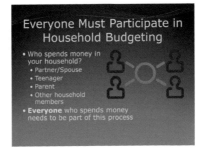

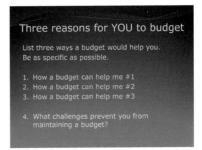

1. http://www.creditloan.com/infographics/how-the-average-consumer-spends-their-paycheck/

although that is the average length of a traditional, fully amortized home loan. If you earmarked $75 for each of your children right now per month and invested it, in 65 years, each would have between $1.5 and $2 million based on the annual collected interest. Detailing your budget will help you prioritize your expenditures. You need to go through your budget with everyone that it covers—your partner and your family, including your children. This is crucial because everyone who is part of the plan must be on board for it to be effective.

A Simple Calculator Helps

Is a calculator required for this class? No, but it certainly helps. If you know how to use spreadsheet or financial software, put that to work for you. The tools are not important. The application and its use are important. You need to find the tools that are comfortable for you and that allow you to track your spending and create a budget that you can follow. Paper, pencil, a calculator, and a record of your spending for the past month is all you really need. Most of us are very bad at guessing what we spend on things; you need to track your spending and use that in your budgeting process.

A Simple Method for Tracking Spending

One way to keep track of what you spend is to label several blank envelopes and with your different spending categories: housing, car, education, clothes, eating out, food, etc. Keep EVERY receipt for a month, and put them in the proper envelopes every night. If you buy something and do not get a receipt, make your own. Write down the amount right away and what it was for and file that away with the rest of your receipts. At the end of the month, total the amount in each envelope and you will have a much better idea of how you actually spend your money.

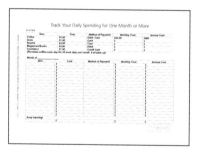

Some people have created a budget using other methods. One way is to label another set of envelopes with your different spending categories, put a dollar figure on the envelope. And put the allotted amount of money for the month in each envelope. That is all that is available to spend on food for the month. If the money runs out within the first couple of weeks of the month, you are spending more than your budgeted amount on food. It is time to make an adjustment and recalculate the budget.

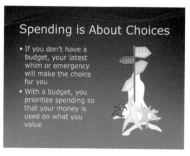

The more detailed your budget, the better off you are going to be. If your budget is not detailed, then you will not really know where your money goes. The budget has to get down to how much you spend on gasoline and oil for your vehicle, how many cups of coffee you buy, the cost of signing your daughter up for soccer, even the cost of picking up your mom's prescription. Little things really do add up. When you run into the drug store or to gas station, do you grab a soda out of the refrigerator, pick up a pack of gum, and snatch a candy bar? If you spend an extra $4 to $5 without noticing it each day, 365 days a year, you would have spent $1,825 by the end of the year with nothing but a few tooth cavities to show for it. Instead, you can choose to save rather than to spend on these items, and you can have the down payment on a home in three to five years.

Think through all your costs in detail. Instead of guessing how much you spend on food, break down the cost by person and per meal. If you have children at home, it costs a minimum of three to four dollars a day per child for lunch, and this needs to be calculated over seven days because the kids eat on the weekends as well as during the week! Here is an example. Use these sample facts, calculate, and see how quickly costs add up.

$4 per day	4 children
7 days a week	4 x 7 x 52 = $1,456 per year per child
52 weeks a year	1,456 ÷ 12 = $121 per month per child
12 months in a year	121 x 4 = $484 per month for four kids

Using this example, $484 a month is spent on feeding four children for lunch only. This is a conservative figure, but probably more than you would have guessed without doing the calculation.

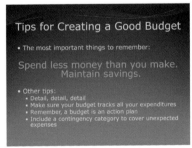

All of us have gone to a fast food restaurant thinking, "Oh, I am just going to spend four or five bucks." The milk shake looks so tasty and the upgrade to the larger fries is so tempting. The next thing you know, ten dollars has disappeared through the drive-thru window. Food costs add up quickly for a family when you factor in adults who eat lunch out. The following is another example calculation: the cost of eating out, even cheaply.

$10 per lunch	1 adult
5 lunches a week	10 x 5 x 50 = $2500 per year
12 months in a year	2500 ÷ 12 = $208 per month for work lunches for EACH adult
50 working weeks a year	

Combine this lunch run through the fast food restaurant with the cost of lunches for four kids and the result is $692 a month, just for lunch. Bringing your lunch to work could easily mean a savings of $2000 a year. Taking your family out to dinner a few times a month can really add up as well.

How much do you spend at the specialized coffee stand on a weekly basis? Do you happen to use the coffee stand as a meeting place? The cost of high-end, convenience coffee adds up very quickly. Buying a $3.25 cup of coffee three times a week adds up to more than $40 a month. You could be saving this much every month towards the down payment on a home or for retirement. It adds up very quickly.

Is anybody surprised at how much going to a movie costs these days? Ticket and concession stand prices at a professional baseball game can also be very high. With a family of four, five or six, it really adds up. Forgoing a twice-a-month movie outing results in an additional $136 a month savings, on average. Staying at home and renting a film starts to look very attractive at that point.

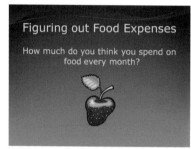

These are just a couple of examples to consider when structuring a budget that works long-term. Think of your own buying habits and figure out how much you could save by spending differently. You may be surprised to find, when you start saving your receipts, that you are not saving properly and are spending money in many frivolous ways. Little adjustments do add up to large savings. Remember, consistency matters, so always be realistic, and do not be too hard on yourself. Simply decide what is most important to you and to your family's future.

● Saving for a Down Payment

The amount required can seem impossible, but it is not insurmountable. Right now in 2011, only one-third of the bank foreclosures in California are actually on the market. Therefore, if you are looking to buy, there will be inventory available for years to come. You can take your time in choosing what you are going to purchase. There is no need to rush! When you purchase a home, closing costs are an additional expense that may be paid by the seller. As more and more homes come on the market, you will have more options and may be able to get the seller to pay for your closing costs.

So, how much monthly income does one need to purchase a $250,000 home? Without considering "other" obligations and just looking at the total housing expense, a household income of $5,800 gross income per month is what one would need. That would leave you $1,800 (31% of $5,300 a month gross income) for principal, interest, taxes and insurance. In addition, a mortgage insurance premium (MIP) is required on an FHA loan. This example provides for $578 for other debt, which could be your car loan and minimum payments on your credit cards. When they are qualifying you for a home loan, lenders do not look at what you actually pay against these bills, they take the minimum payment required. This fact is very important to note. If you are truly following your budget and acting in your family's best interest, you will be paying more than the minimum payments on your debt and will thus have less available for your monthly mortgage payment. This is one reason why you may not want to accept a mortgage at the highest monthly payment for which you are qualified.

Compound Interest

What can those dollars do for you? If you start cutting back on expenses, like eating lunch out, you can save a lot of money very quickly. Watch what those dollars can do in a relatively short period. Let us use the example of $100 a month in savings over five years. With 3% interest, putting $100 a month away would result in more than $6,400 at the end of five years. If you put

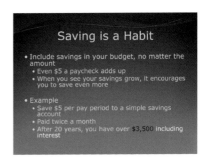

away $150 a month, you would have more than $9,600 at the end of five years. That is enough for a 3.5% down payment on an FHA loan with a little left over. In fact, the $6,400 could be a down payment for an $180,000 house in today's market. Why wait five years? If you are tight on your budget, and save aggressively putting away $200 a month, after only three years you would have more than $7,500. The point is that compound interest makes your money grow at a faster rate. This is why you need to start saving NOW. What does buying below your means and saving more for your retirement mean to you? If you start saving $100 a month when you are 20 years old at 8% interest, you will have $530,970 by the time you are 65. Saving $200 per month with the same factors results in $1,061,940. Start saving now!

Take the average household income for the western part of the United States that was noted above: $68,000. That income could qualify for a $250,000 loan amount with only 3.5% down with today's FHA financing standards. The required down payment would be $8,750. In three to four years, a $150- to $200-a-month savings in your budget will result in enough money for a down payment.

The American Dream of Home Ownership

Be realistic when you are creating your budget. If you are too hard on yourself when creating your spending plan, you will never be able to stick with it. Simply decide what is most important to you.

❓ Ask the Expert

Question: How do you deal with—or prevent—major financial catastrophes?

Answer: Because unexpected events can put a strain on finances, the best way to avoid letting these events become financial catastrophes is to plan ahead. Here is a story to illustrate this point.

> When I was very young and moved out of the house, my dad said, "Hey, I want to take you to lunch." He sat down across a table and said, "Listen, son, if you get injured and you are lying on a curb, your mother is going to make me take care of you." I thought that was funny because that is just my dad's sense of humor. However, he explained the need for me to have insurance because it would not be fair for me to put that added burden on my mother and father.

The way to handle catastrophes, frankly, is to plan and make sure your budget includes insurance. Saving as much as possible helps too, of course, but insurance is the best way that you can cover yourself because most of us do not have a lot left over after covering living costs.

Loan originators often do not factor in the expense of insurance. Before saying yes to a loan, look at your whole picture. Did you factor in lost income insurance? Did you factor in medical insurance? Did you factor in your deductible? Did you factor in co-payments? What about life insurance or a term policy to cover the amount of the mortgage? There are so many details that your lender is not going to ask. Having the right insurance and making sure you do not get into a financial situation where you cannot pay your insurance is the best way to protect yourself from financial disasters.

How many believe that the American Dream has always been to own a home? We have been taught that the American Dream is homeownership. While homeownership is a worthy goal and has many benefits for both the individual and our communities, it is far more important to make sure that you have successfully budgeted to maintain shelter. We have learned that people buying homes in 2003 to 2007 suffered great losses in the values of their homes. Instead of being the American Dream, for many it became the American nightmare, and many people were left without places to live. Therefore, it is crucial that you learn to budget to at least maintain shelter, before you focus on budgeting to buy real estate for investment purposes. If your goals and your finances permit, it can be both, but primarily Americans need to focus on having a roof over their heads for their family.

● Rent vs. Own. Which Is Best for You?

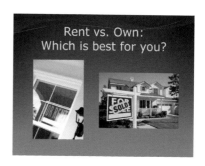

For some people, entertainment, travel and vacation are more important than having a home. Perhaps you have hobbies or other activities that drive you to avoid becoming house poor. Do you want the responsibility of owning a home? No? That is OK. The purpose of this course is not to pressure people into buying a house. There are many reasons to believe in and aspire toward home ownership, but it is not for everyone. Perhaps you cannot afford a home at this time because you are living in a situation where the cost just to get by does not allow the ability to save for a down payment. If that is the case, just make sure that you budget and save enough to keep your roof over your head, and put the prospect of home ownership on the back burner until circumstances change.

Unexpected Expenses

If you have elderly parents, you may need to consider their needs when budgeting and buying. We have seen first-hand that many people will buy a home without considering that their mother or father may need additional care five to six years down the road. Little can cause more stress and strife on a family than when your partner's parents need care and you have failed to prepare for this additional loved one being in the home or the expense that goes along with caring for them. That can be extremely costly and painful for a family. Many of us will need to take care of our parents, so generational planning should be an important part of your budget.

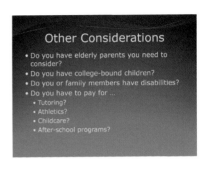

College-Bound Children

Do you have college-bound children? Do you have adults or children in your home with disabilities? Do your children desire additional tutoring, enrichment programs, or after-school activities? The out-of-pocket costs skyrocket when you start factoring in baseball, soccer, dance lessons, and piano. These are all additional expenses that underwriters do not include when calculating an affordable monthly house payment. However, these expenses are real and therefore you must factor them into your budget.

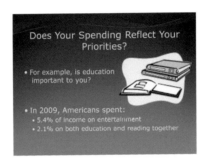

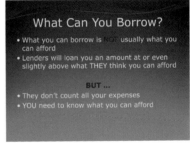

Family Lifestyle Matters

Do not allow somebody to convince you that lifestyle expenses are not important, and all that matters is simply qualifying for a loan. These expenses may not factor into your qualification in the lend-

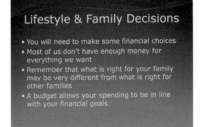

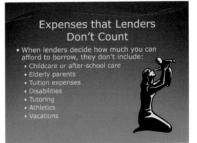

er's automated software, but they are hugely important for a happy and stable home life. Ensure you can continue to afford these expenditures as well as a house payment. Always factor what matters to you into your budget in order to maintain peace and decrease stress in the household. Factor in family needs and activities into any budget to avoid increased financial pressures on you and your loved ones down the road.

Tax Benefits of Owning a Home

The question of renting versus buying weighs the benefit of less responsibility for the renter against tax benefits and potential appreciation for the homeowner. In the United States, the tax benefits for home ownership are dramatic. Homeownership is the last great tax write-off we have. One hundred percent of your mortgage interest is tax-deductible on IRS Form 1040, Schedule A. The United States Congress is talking about changing a few things for incomes above $250,000, so the benefit

may change for those at that income level. But right now, for most of us, all one hundred cents of the dollar that you spend on mortgage interest is deductible. If you become a homeowner, you are going to learn about line 10 of your Schedule A and be very excited about that particular line. On a $200,000 loan at 5.5% interest, that is almost $10,000 taken straight off your income for tax purposes. How much you save on your taxes depends on your tax bracket and a few other factors. For more details contact the IRS at 1-800-829-1040 and they will answer your basic questions. Or, you may wish to visit www.irs.gov and search for Publication 936 to read about the mortgage interest deduction.

Value Appreciation

Over long periods of time, home values have typically gone up. The percentage depends on multiple factors, with the most weight placed on location. But many people have recently experienced that what goes up can definitely come down. When you own a home, your property may decrease in value due to market devaluation; this is what happens when the overall value of the housing market goes down as it did from 2007 to 2011. This is different from physical depreciation, where a home loses value because of its physical condition. Homeownership became a nightmare for many people, not the dream they had hoped if they bought at the peak of the real estate market only to have their home's market value decrease by 50%. However, for those of you thinking about buying in the next three to five years or sooner, you will look back on this time and reflect that this was the greatest housing market opportunity ever.

Ask the Expert

Question: Would you tell someone that owns multiple units and their own home to budget the same way as someone who is just buying their first home?

Answer: The short answer is, yes. However, a more detailed answer is that it depends on the cash flow of the unit(s). If a property enjoys a positive cash flow, meaning the rent received is greater than the overall expenses, you may not have to set as much aside. Regardless, average maintenance must be factored into the budget to avoid surprises and costly deferred maintenance.

Most people with investment properties are showing a loss on their IRS Form 1040 Schedule E, which is a profit and loss statement for investment properties. Why? They are not budgeting enough for maintenance and the deferred maintenance eventually catches up to them. One of the things you will learn in our "Borrowing" chapter is the importance of budgeting for maintenance of the units or your own personal residence. Budgeting for maintenance costs is not required to get a home loan, but if you do not save for regular maintenance on your properties, you will find yourself like many investors who cannot turn a profit or homeowners who must put off replacing carpet, repainting and other important things that help keep your home (or investment property) beautiful and enjoyable.

Experts say homeowners need to set between 1.5% and 2% of the acquisition price of a property aside to cover regular maintenance costs. We recommend setting aside 1.75% of the acquisition price (divided by twelve) monthly for maintenance. In an investment property, things break or renters trash a unit and you have to repaint and re-carpet. Proper budgeting and consistency matters whether you are talking about units, a rental property, or your own personal residence. It is all the same.

If you are going to buy, now is the time to do it. Interest rates are still at historical lows. They are presently artificially low in order to stimulate growth. When the economy improves and this stimulation is no longer needed, there will

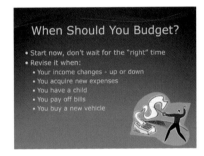

most assuredly be an increase in interest rates. A small change in interest will result in a huge difference in overall cost to the buyer. If you wait for another few years to buy, the difference between a 5% interest rate and a 7% interest rate on a $250,000 loan is over $115,000 in additional interest. In addition, the difference for a borrower who qualifies for a $250,000 mortgage at 7% is approximately $49,000 less purchasing power than a loan at 5%. The days of 15-20% appreciation per year on the value of your house are over, but a more realistic 3% to 4% appreciation is going to be likely. That means that over time, the value of your home will increase, but not dramatically. Although you should consider the financial benefits that can result from homeownership, owning a home should be a personal choice first and an investment second.

Module 2: Borrowing

• A Complex Topic

Loans and borrowing are very complex topics, because important information about them is changing all the time and there is a lot of information out there. Real estate professionals, loan officers, loan originators and agents have an obligation to understand the ethical issues surrounding the borrowing process. These are the professionals that you must rely on to complete your purchase. Unfortunately, many homeowners who lost their homes during the foreclosure crisis discovered that there are unqualified and/or unethical professionals who can mislead you. This section of the guide will help you devise interview questions to test your real estate professional's ethics and knowledge. In addition, you will ground yourself in realistic borrowing expectations.

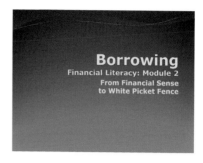

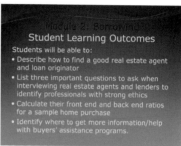

• An Emotional Decision

Most homeowners choose a home based on emotions first and then rationalize or justify the purchase price second. That is just human nature. Builders know this and use your emotional attachment to their advantage. Have you ever been in a model home? What do people do? They admire the model home and say, "This is beautiful! Look at how perfectly this beautiful big screen TV fits in the living room." Next, you look through the glass door into the backyard and see a beautiful barbecue with a pizza oven. "I cannot wait to have a barbecue in this back yard." You visualize yourself living there. There is a reason why builders take a $250,000 model home and load it with $100,000 in upgrades. The builder wishes you to visualize yourself living there and it works! How many of us can purchase a home and decorate to that degree all at one time? Once you see a property and become emotionally attached, you may be tempted to purchase it, even if you really cannot afford it. Budget first, and then borrow.

After you create a budget, know your spending patterns, and have a very good idea what you can afford for a down payment and closing costs, then you are ready to buy. When we make emotional decisions about buying a house, we often make bad financial decisions. Take the emotion out of the equation until you qualify for an appropriate loan that you can afford and still live comfortably. Then go out looking at houses. Your first step should be to find out information on the loan.

With just a few subtle changes in your spending choices, you can make a difference in whether you retire in comfort, or like most, struggle. Plan ahead and stick to your plan. Set yourself apart and focus on long-term goals rather than short-term emotional choices.

We have seen a lot of carnage occur in our economy when the public is not well-informed and financially literate. When you learn how to borrow and how not to borrow, you are equipping yourself, your family, and your neighbors for success. We are all in this together.

• Saving For a Home

How can you save for a home? Decide what you want and what you are willing to sacrifice. There are four keys to success.

1. Decide what you want

2. Decide what you are willing to give up for it

3. Set your priorities, and

4. Go to work.

How Can I Save For A Home?
- First, decide what you need and want in a home
- Second, determine what you can sacrifice financially to obtain your desired home

Create a Plan
- Determine down payment
- Determine closing costs
- Determine maintenance expenses
- Save for reserves too!

Deciding what you want can be challenging. You will have to establish your priorities. What are you willing to sacrifice? Is the sacrifice worth it to become a homeowner? You may decide it is not. However, if you become a homeowner, there will be benefits. If buying your own home is important to you, then let us figure out how to do it: the down payment, closing costs, maintenance costs, and reserves.

• Find the Right Professionals to Help

Find the Right Professionals
- Two types of professionals will play key roles in your borrowing and purchasing experience
  - Real Estate Agent
  - Loan Originator
- Do NOT work with an unqualified professional. These experts are the ones who determine the home you purchase and the loan you obtain.
- Talk to AT LEAST TWO loan originators and AT LEAST TWO real estate agents before deciding who to hire.

Two professionals will play a key role in your borrowing and purchasing experience, your real estate agent and your loan originator. These experts make sure that you obtain the home and loan that you want. Finding high-quality, experienced professionals with strong professional ethics is essential to ensure you end up with a home you love, but also can afford. Do not sacrifice anything in this regard, especially ethics in your real estate professional. An ethical but inexperienced professional can always seek guidance from more experienced professionals, but an unethical professional is downright dangerous.

You are hiring these professionals to help you find and afford a home. You should talk to AT LEAST TWO loan originators and AT LEAST TWO real estate agents before deciding whom to work with. Below are several helpful questions to use when interviewing real estate professionals. Listen to what they say, how well they explain things, and how well they listen to you. If something about that person does not feel quite right, do not work with them.

How Do I Find a Qualified Loan Originator?

The first real estate professional you meet in the process of getting a loan is your loan originator. This person can make or break this process. Your loan originator should be knowledgeable, willing to listen, and able to help you get approved for a loan that fits within your budget. Use your budget to regulate your desire to overspend. Do not work with someone who tries to talk you into more than you can afford. A good loan originator is a person who truly cares about you and is going to provide good counsel. You as a consumer should require these attributes of all your professionals. She or he will talk to you about realistic expectations. Once you find a good loan originator, one who cares and looks out for you, stay loyal to that person forever!

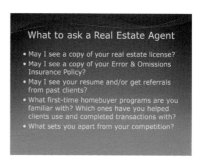

There are many questions you may wish to ask bankers, loan originators, mortgage bankers, or mortgage brokers before deciding with whom to work. Here are several important questions that you should ask.

- May I see a copy of your real estate license and proof of your Mortgage Loan Originator License Endorsement Certificate? Both of these are legal requirements for loan originators and you can look up their status by clicking here: http://www.nmlsconsumeraccess.org/.

- May I see a copy of your errors and omissions insurance policy? Optional: he/she may be self-insured.

- May I see your resume and/or get referrals from past clients?

- With which first-time homebuyer programs are you familiar? Which programs have you helped clients use and with which have you completed transactions?

5. Are there any financial, marketing, or commission arrangements between you and the professionals to whom you are referring me?

What Should I Ask Before Hiring My Real Estate Agent?

There are many important questions you should consider when selecting a real estate professional, in addition to considering your impressions of how he or she treats you during the interview. Among those questions are the following:

- May I see a copy of your real estate license?

- May I see a copy of your errors and omissions insurance policy?

- May I see your resume and/or receive referrals from past clients?

- With which first-time homebuyer programs are you familiar? Which transactions have you helped clients use and complete?

- What sets you apart from your competition?

- Do you or your company receive any additional monies or referral fees for directing me to a lender, title, or escrow company? This must be disclosed in writing.

• What Is in a Payment?

Your monthly payment will have at least four major parts: principal, interest, taxes and insurance (PITI). If you buy a condominium or home with a homeowners association (HOA), this may also be included in your monthly payment. There may also be private mortgage insurance (PMI) or a mortgage insurance premium (MIP) included in your monthly payments, as required for those putting less than 20% down on a home loan, or receiving an FHA loan. In California, many homes have municipal bonds

that are attached (this is called a lien) to the home and are collected through the county tax collector. These are commonly referred to as Mello-Roos taxes or bonds, named after State Senator Henry Mello and Assembly member Mike Roos, who authored the Community Facilities District Act of 1982. These can be for a fixed period of time, but in some cases they are perpetual. Ask about them and fully understand how they will impact your payments, now and in the future. Many people have lost their homes because they did not fully understand that these taxes can dramatically increase your monthly house payment. Sadly, many loan professionals are not familiar with this area of their business.

Which mortgage insurance policy may be required, if any, depends on your type of loan. Pour over your "good faith estimate" and be sure your loan originator can answer the questions, "Who, when, and why?" for each individual line item on the estimate. Who is charging the fee? When does it apply and why am I charged the fee? You have a right to ask and understand the answers to these questions.

An easy mnemonic for remembering the components of your monthly payment is PITI.

- P Principal: The principal is the amount of money that you borrowed that is still unpaid.

- I Interest: A large portion of your monthly payment will be interest. At the beginning of your loan, you will pay far more toward interest than principal.

- T Taxes Property: taxes only

- I Insurance: Fire/hazard insurance only

Ask the Expert

Question: Is a mortgage tri-merge report the same credit report that the automobile industry uses in order to determine creditworthiness?

Answer: Yes and no. It is coming from the same sources, but a mortgage lender or a bank will pull your credit in a different way. Lenders have their own way of doing business and so that is why, if you are going to be buying a home, it is worth it to invest that $13–$15 to get a tri-merge report.

Property Taxes

You will pay a percentage of the assessed value of your house to your local county assessor's office every year. The assessed value of your house is often based on the acquisition price. However, it does not have to be. The assessor determines value every January in California and the tax collector is bound to collect taxes based on this assessment. It matters not what your loan or real estate professionals tell you. You must go directly to the county in which your property resides and contact the tax collectors office in order to determine your tax liability. You will get two tax bills your first year, one is paid as part of the closing costs, in the same amount that the seller would have paid. The second is a special assessment that is a correction or addition to make up for any difference between what you owe in property taxes and the rate the seller was paying.

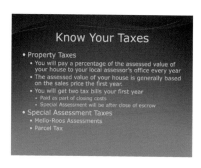

Know your property taxes and break them down for the properties you are considering. The county tax assessor's records are open for viewing. You can always contact the assessor through e-mail to request a breakdown of the taxes for a given property. You need to know all the taxes, including those for lighting, landscaping, mosquito abatement, and school bonds. Ensure your loan originator considers any additional taxes when estimating your monthly payment.

Proposition 13

In 1978, California voters passed Proposition 13, which limits how much your property taxes can go up each year. Under Proposition 13, the annual increase to your property taxes cannot be more than 2%. It also limits the tax rate to 1% of the property value plus what is required to pay voter-approved assessment bonds.[2]

---

2. http://www.boe.ca.gov/proptaxes/faqs/caproptaxprop.htm#2

Mello-Roos

As mentioned earlier, in 1978, Senator Henry Mello and Assembly member Mike Roos carried the Community Facilities District Act of 1982 (Mello-Roos) in California to help create a funding mechanism for developing neighborhoods. A lot of infrastructure and other improvements are required in order to create a new and safe development. These bonds are a vehicle for communities to fund these improvements. Bonds are paid over a 15-, 20-, or 30-year period. Assessments are not based on individual home values, but are assessed per parcel. If there is a $3,000–$4,000 annual tax that has to be collected per parcel, it will be collected whether or not your loan originator and real estate agent told you about it. People can get behind in their mortgages if Mello-Roos bonds are not taken into account when calculating the monthly "PITI." It is important to understand that regardless of the assessed value of one's home, these fixed bonds must be collected. Therefore, even if the assessor reduces your home's value to $1.00, but you have a $4,000 annual bond payment that is due, this fixed bond payment will not change based on the home's value and will be collected irrespective of the home's value. A lender may pay these taxes and then increase monthly payments to cover them. Sometimes it is more than a homeowner can sustain. If the homeowner can barely afford his or her house payments already, adding another $300 or $400 dollars a month on top of that payment makes it impossible. Do not be caught off guard. Contact the tax collector's or tax assessor's office for the county in which you are going to buy and confirm what your obligations will be before closing on your home purchase.

The Loan Process

To get a loan, the first step is qualification. There are two parts to qualification. First, you must qualify for a loan. Second, the property you wish to purchase must also qualify for the loan. To determine if you qualify for a loan, the

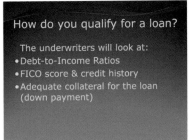

lender will look at your income, credit score and your financial situation using a set of ratios.

Qualifying Ratios

Ratios are how a lender measures and gains comfort that you can make your monthly obligations. There are two ratios that the lender will calculate when you apply for a loan: the front-end ratio and the back-end ratio.

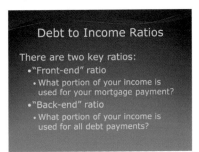

Front-End Ratio

The front-end ratio, also known as the housing ratio, is a calculated numerical factor. We are going to use round numbers to make the calculation examples easy. Let us assume your total gross monthly income is $4,000. Lenders always use your gross income in their calculations (unless you are self-employed); this is your income before taxes and any withholdings from your paycheck. Let us assume the proposed monthly housing payment (PITI) is $1,000.

Calculating "Front-End" Ratio

Front-end example:
- Total monthly mortgage payment = $1,000
- Total monthly gross income = $4,000

$1,000/$4,000= 0.25

Front-end ratio = 25%

$$\text{Front-End Ratio} = \frac{Housing\ payment}{Gross\ income} = \frac{\$1,000}{\$4,000} = 0.25 = 25\%$$

Back-End Ratio

The back-end ratio, also known as the debt ratio, is also a numerical factor. This ratio demonstrates your total monthly debt obligations as a percentage of your income. We will use the proposed monthly mortgage payment of $1,000 and then add your car payment, minimum payment on your revolving debt such as your credit card, and maybe a student loan, for another $500 a month. That totals $1,500. Here is the calculation.

Calculating "Back-End" Ratio

Back-end Example:

- Total monthly loan payments of all kinds (including mortgage) = $1,500
- Total monthly gross income = $4,000

$1,500/$4,000 = .375

Back-end ratio = 37.5%

$$\text{Back-End Ratio} = \frac{Monthly\ debt\ payment}{Gross\ income} = \frac{\$1,500}{\$4,000} = 0.375 = 37.5\%$$

Therefore, the front-end is your housing and the back-end includes all other debt. In your actual spending, you know that you have to factor in everything. You have your minimum payments on your credit cards and student loans, but you have probably decided it is in your best interest to pay more than your minimum payment on these debts each month. These additional payments are not counted in these ratios and this is exactly why your personal budget is so crucial—so that when your lender

Overall Debt Ratios

According to Example:
- Front-end/Back-end
- 25%/37.5%
- These ratios are good ones that should qualify for a loan

calculates your possible monthly payment, you will know more about your financial situation and what you can really afford.

The average back-end ratio today of people asking for a modified loan is 79.8, meaning that about 80% of that family's budget is going to loan payments, with only 20% left for food, healthcare, transportation and all other expenses. Recent numbers show[3] the average back-end ratio after borrowers receive a loan modification is 63.5%, far too high to expect much success in repayment.

---

3. www.financialstability.gov

If you came to a lender, asked for a loan, and received that loan with a 55% back-end ratio, that would be considered predatory lending by most standards. This is the reason you are seeing 50% of people fall out of their modifications in the first 12 months, and 60–70% fall out within 24 months; a loan with a 63.5% back-end ratio is just not sustainable. The ratios in this example, 25% and 37.5%, are great. You should easily qualify for a loan with these ratios, and would likely be able to make the payments.

• Do You Understand Your FICO Score?

Your FICO or credit score is also important in qualifying for a loan. You need to have a 640 or higher FICO score to be eligible for a loan. FICO is an acronym for Fair Isaac and Company, the entity that created a computer algorithm to predict someone's likelihood of repaying a loan. There are three major credit reporting agencies: Equifax, Experian, and TransUnion. A little known fact is that the three companies use FICO. They do so under different brand names, but it is all FICO. In fact, if everybody reported the exact same information to all three bureaus, your score would be the same with all three bureaus. However, this is not what tends to happen. Some information is reported to one bureau, some to another. Lenders will look at scores from all three credit bureaus and use the middle score. Lenders take the middle of the three scores as very few lenders report to all three bureaus at the same time. That is why the scores can vary greatly. Getting that FICO score of 640 or higher is very, very crucial. In addition, the higher the score, the better the interest rate you will be able to get.

> ### Your Credit (FICO) Score
>
> - FICO scores range from 300-850 points
> - 640 or higher is the goal
> - Requesting your score too much can lower it
> - Avoiding credit score pitfalls

How Can You Raise Your FICO Score?

Here is some basic information about FICO scores and some tips on how to make sure your FICO score stays high. Scores are updated on a regular basis; usually the score model changes about every 45 days. Everyone is entitled under federal statutes to one free credit report[4] from each bureau every year. There are many for-profit companies that will provide your credit report, but they will not give you your FICO score without payment. The FDIC recommends using www.annualcreditreport.com to check your credit score.

If you want to be a qualified buyer, be willing to spend $13–$15 to have a qualified loan originator pull a "tri-merge report." That is the report that lenders are going to look at. If you show your lender a report from just one bureau, say TransUnion, they will look at it and say, "Thanks. I need to run my own report." You need to know your middle FICO score so you can see if there is anything to repair in order to improve your score.

If you are preparing to buy a house, you want to be very careful about anything having to do with your credit. Do NOT go out and get a new credit card to buy furniture while you are in the process of getting your loan. Even though you have been approved, if any of your information changes, you can be denied the loan up until the actual closing.

Many people cause problems in their loan approval process because they do not understand how credit works. If a potential borrower calls the credit card company for an interest reduction, the company does a "soft pull." You did not see them pull your credit. You did not give authorization to pull your credit. Nevertheless, the credit card company checks your credit. While they are checking, they see an unpaid collection account for your old cell phone company because you moved a couple of times and you owe $186. It is an unpaid collection account. What does the credit card company do? They say, "Oh. We need to update our records." Adding that unpaid collection account will take your score from the 640 you had down to 620 or lower. Now, you no longer get to buy that home without first improving your score. Make sure that you work with an expert that understands FICO scores and how they work.

Lenders want to see that you have the ability to borrow and pay back. To that end, they want to see that you have at least three credit lines and some other line of credit such as an auto loan, that are seasoned, meaning you have had them a while. Ideally, lenders wish to see a high credit limit of $2,500 for typically three to four years. Having less than three cards is not good because it shows that you may not be qualified to get credit. Having more than five is also not good; that is too much other credit. Three to five available resources for credit is best. Perhaps you only borrowed

---

4.https://www.annualcreditreport.com/

$200 and paid it back over two or three months. That will actually raise your score. In addition, keeping the balances on those credit cards at 30% or less of your available credit is crucial.

• Check Your Available Credit. Is This A Problem?

Again, with our current system of credit, some things can occur that are actually beyond your ability to control. Lenders are challenged and continually review all of their borrowers and re-evaluate their credit limits. Let us say that you have a credit card that has an available credit limit of $10,000. You owe $3,000. You are right at the 30% and are pre-approved for a home loan. You look at 20 properties and have an accepted contract on one. You are in the third week of a four-week escrow. In the meantime, the bank that issues your credit card happens to be doing their regular review and they note, "Ah. This person is not historically using all $10,000 of that credit limit." The credit card company has the right (found in that tiny print disclosure statement that they send you) to drop your $10,000 available credit down to $6,000. Immediately your balance just went from 30% to 50% of your available credit, and you did not charge a dime. However, this dropped your FICO score down by 20–30 points, or more. Your credit is checked once more just before the loan is funded. Now your score may be lower, so you may not qualify for the loan and you may not close escrow. Husband your credit carefully.

Does getting a loan seem complicated? It can be. This is why you need a trustworthy professional helping you through the process. Finance and credit ratings as well as the lender guidelines are constantly changing. You need to have somebody who is right there on the cutting edge of credit evaluation, and who is paying attention to your needs and situation. You want somebody reading the Fannie Mae (FNMA), Freddie Mac (FDMC), and Department of Housing and Urban Development (HUD) guidelines on a regular basis to make sure that they can advise you properly.

• Automated Underwriting Systems and Qualifying for a Loan

Over 95% of homebuyers will finance their next home purchase. Most of these loans will go through one of a few automated underwriting systems (AUS).[5] In other words, when you talk to a loan originator, some will ask you just a few questions, run those through their system, and give you a pre-approval amount. Does this mean that you will actually be able to get this loan? Perhaps, depending on the details of your personal financial situation and

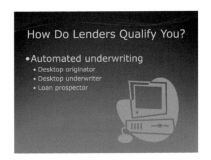

How Do Lenders Qualify You?
•Automated underwriting
  • Desktop originator
  • Desktop underwriter
  • Loan prospector

---

5. Fannie Mae uses the Desktop Originator (DO) and Desktop Underwriter (DU). Freddie Mac uses the Loan Prospector (LP) automated engine.

the details the originator went into during their interview. Remember, this is an automated system and it is wise to recall the adage, "garbage in, garbage out."

Let us look at Barbara as an example. Barbara is a schoolteacher. Her loan originator, Steve, has only been in the business for three or four years, and has not carefully read the HUD form 4155 underwriting criteria for the loan Barbara is applying for. Steve looks at Barbara's paycheck stub, and determines her income. He then types that into the Desktop Originator engine on his computer. The automated engine runs Barbara's credit and merges it with the information Steve has entered. Thirty seconds later, Steve says, "Congratulations, Barbara! You are approved for a home loan!"

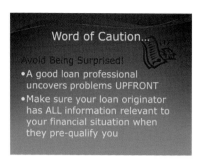

Word of Caution...
Avoid Being Surprised!
•A good loan professional uncovers problems UPFRONT
•Make sure your loan originator has ALL information relevant to your financial situation when they pre-qualify you

Barbara and her real estate agent spend the next two months searching like crazy to find a home and she is finally in contract with an accepted offer. She calls Steve back to say, "Hey, I found a home." Steve dusts off her approval. Now that they are closer to actually doing the loan, Steve enters in the rest of her information, updating her supporting information. Then the underwriter, who looks carefully at all of Barbara's financials and must approve the loan, and who reads all the underwriting criteria, looks at it and says to Steve, "I hope you did not tell her that she has an approval. When you submitted the loan package, you indicated her teacher's income on a 10-month contract, not a 12-month contract, So the annual income listed is incorrect. The teacher is paid the amount indicated on the pay stub for 10 months of the year, not 12. In addition, tax returns show that Barbara spends money out of her own pocket on the classroom, as do many schoolteachers. Teachers are infrequently reimbursed for out-of-pocket expenses and her tax pre-parer filed IRS Form 2106 for un-reimbursed employee business expenses in order to reduce her tax liability. By doing so, her income is reduced and should have been factored in at the time of the application. Loan declined."

What happened? Barbara is able to write off $250.00 in the year 2010 from her personal taxes on IRS Form 2106 for those out-of-pocket amounts that she spends on her classroom. The underwriter factors that in as a debt over a 24-month average, but Steve, the loan originator, did not count that. Barbara has been approved for the loan in her mind for the last three months. She has shopped. Her real estate agent has been looking at homes. The sellers of the home she wanted to buy said to themselves, "Oh great! We just sold our home, and now we can go ahead and give a non-refundable deposit on that property in the next state because we want to be with our grandkids." Unfortunately, the deal falls apart, and everyone plans to sue because the loan originator did not know what he was doing. Ignorance is not bliss. When you find a good loan originator, hang on to him or her, and reward him or her with your loyalty. A good loan professional uncovers virtually all problems upfront. Steve should have pulled information from Barbara's tax returns and gone through the application with her line by line to be sure that he had included everything in the pre-approval process.

Ability to Borrow and Willingness to Repay

Lenders must be able to verify two items about you. First, can you demonstrate ability to repay the loan through your job and your savings? Secondly, what is your willingness to repay debt, as reflected by your credit report?

Qualifying Made Simple

- What lenders are really looking for is:
  1. Ability to repay debt
  2. Willingness to repay debt

Documentation

When you meet with a lender to determine if you qualify for a loan, you are going to need 30 days of paycheck stubs and two years of W-2s and tax returns including all schedules. You want the lender to consider your tax returns because you want them to determine any challenges at the beginning of the process. You do not have to provide paper copies of your tax returns

What you will need:

- 30 days of paychecks
- 2 years of W-2s & tax returns
  Information on all other assets
  - Checking statements
  - Savings statements
  - Retirement statements
  - Funds must be sourced and seasoned for 60 days

to get a home loan today. You can authorize your loan originator using IRS Form 4506-T to pull your electronic tax returns, but a quality loan professional will wish to review your tax returns themselves, upfront, in order to avoid challenges down the road. Keep in mind, IRS Form 4506-T can provide an unlimited authorization. Be wise. Make sure the document you sign approving access provides for the years required to obtain your loan and no more.

Here is another industry tip. If you do your own taxes, have a professional review your tax returns before you apply for the loan. If you are self-employed, make sure that you get somebody who is qualified to look at your IRS Schedule C, IRS Form K-1, your partnerships, your IRS Form 1120, and other relevant forms. All of that information is crucial to the loan qualification process and you do not want to find a problem down the road that can be resolved now.

You are going to need records for all your assets including your checking, savings and retirement information. If you have a quarterly statement for your retirement that reads, "Page 1 of 4" and page 4 is blank, you still need the blank page. If the underwriter sees there are four pages to a document, four pages must be provided. News reports claim that there is more loan fraud committed in California and Florida than in the rest of the United States combined. Thus, you must be able to support your claims with empirical evidence.

The same holds true with your checking and savings account information. You need to have two months of statements, but bring three. If questions arise and you are asked for more documentation—have it ready. This will make the process move smoothly.

Budget Letter

Underwriters know that very few people bother to budget or to do what you have done and take a class like this. Thus, you should submit a budget letter with your application. From an underwriting

? Ask the Expert

Question: How can we help our parents if they are considering a reverse mortgage?

Answer: Consider contacting the U.S. Department of Housing and Urban Development (HUD). Their web site is http://www.hud.gov. This is the actual government department monitoring and insuring the program. Get the proper counseling. You may wish to contact the National Foundation for Credit Counselors (NFCC) http://www.nfcc.org. These credit counselors are specifically trained to assist you in matters of credit and financing. You can contact either organization directly through its website, and you will be referred o appropriate counselors in your neighborhood, at no cost to you. You and your parents can actually sit down with an HUD-approved counselor paid by the government to counsel you on your rights and the responsibilities of reverse mortgage loans. You will get everything in writing, too.

perspective, a good budget letter is like gold. Include a certificate of participation from a class like this or a similar homebuyer-training program. Create the budget we have worked on in the first module of this class, and include a copy with a letter describing why you are interested in becoming a homeowner. This is a "motivation letter." Document that you can afford this home, with money left over. If you have factored in maintenance and savings, the lender will be very excited about wanting to approve you for a loan.

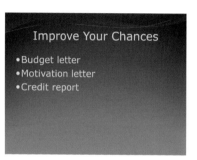

• Credit Report

Explain everything on your credit report. If there is anything derogatory (negative) you will need to document what happened, no matter how old the credit item is. Handwrite a story about what occurred. Industry professionals know that most derogatory letters are written by the loan professional. The borrowers see most of these letters for the first time when they are signing their closing documents. Underwriters realize this, so when a letter is submitted to them unsigned and will then scrutinize loans much more. You want the underwriter to know YOU wrote it. Handwrite it, sign it and make it part of your loan submission.

• Credit Inquiries

Document those unexplained credit inquires for those occasions where your credit report has been pulled. As an example, if the underwriter sees a credit inquiry from a Ford Motor Corporation, he or she may be very nervous and anxious. This is an indication that you may be buying a car during the loan process or shortly thereafter. The lender will scrutinize your loan even more.

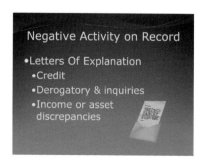

You want to be able to explain in writing that you just happened to be shopping with a friend. You gave the salesperson your driver's license and your credit was pulled without you knowing. Assure the lender that you are not planning to buy a car.

Down Payment and Asset Discrepancies

You need to show you have the money available for your down payment and your closing costs. This is best accomplished with copies of your savings, where money has been in the account for at least 60 days. Lender underwriting guidelines require down payment funds to be "seasoned" for a minimum of 60 days. If the money is coming from a source that is a little bit hard to document, make sure you explain this upfront. You must also document the source and ability of the donor if you are receiving any gift funds from family or friends. In addition, you will need to provide an appropriate gift letter stating that the funds are in fact a gift towards the purchase of your home and are not to be repaid. Document your income, alimony, second job, everything upfront even though you may not have to provide the actual proof until the last second of the loan process. A good loan officer will always ask for more documentation than they will need in order to determine if there are any possible challenges that need to be addressed upfront to avoid surprises at the end.

Good Faith Estimate—How Does It Work?

Within three business days of applying for a loan, your lender must provide you with a good faith estimate of the fees and costs associated with that loan. The good faith estimate is considered a guarantee thanks to changes in consumer protection law effective January 10, 2010. Today,

a lender who puts the rate, terms, and fees in writing is committed to it. Be sure and have your professional go over all of the laws that have recently passed due to the financial crisis. Any changes in fees, rates, or terms no matter how small will require a new updated good faith estimate and a delay in closing. In some cases, the loan officer will have to absorb costs, as these costs cannot change even with a new disclosure. Visit www.hud.gov and search "good faith estimate" to learn more.

• Qualifying—The Property

What is LTV? Your loan originator will probably talk about LTV— your loan-to-value ratio. This is a measurement of how much of the value of the property is borrowed. Most conventional lenders want to see an LTV that is 80% or lower. Here is an example.

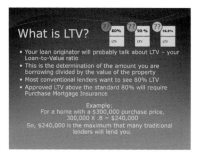

For a home with a $300,000 purchase price:

$$LTV = \$300{,}000 \times 0.8 = \$240{,}000$$

In this example, $240,000 is the maximum that many traditional lenders will lend you on a home with a purchase price of $300,000. Lenders will lend more as long as there is private mortgage insurance to cover them in the event of a future loss. Prior to the financial crisis, private mortgage insurance was often replaced with home equity lines of credit that funded along with the 80% first trust deed to create a combined loan to value. However, with the current adverse market conditions, this is no longer an option offered most borrowers. Once again, private mortgage insurance is used to allow borrowers to qualify for a loan with less than 20% down payment.

• Appraised Values

The property also has to qualify, or pass approval, for the loan. Lenders may not want to make a loan on a property in poor condition, or may require certain repairs before approval of the loan. You may want to evaluate and consider the overall condition of the property if you are purchasing a fixer-upper. A property that requires extensive repairs may cause the loan to be denied. The lender will also order an appraisal, an official statement of the value of the property. The appraised value must be

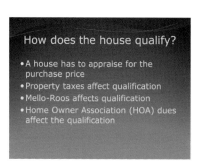

at least the purchase price on the home, or the lender may require you to make up the difference in cash. However, if this affects a borrower's financial reserves used to approve them in the first place, the lender may not allow this additional contribution. A lender will only lend a percentage of the purchase price or the appraised value, whichever is less."

What Else Affects Loan Qualifications?

Property taxes, Mello-Roos taxes, and homeowners association dues (HOA) affect qualifications. Therefore, you may qualify for a certain loan amount, and shop for homes in that price range, but find a house that has an HOA. You need to go back to your loan officer to find out how much you qualify for when the HOA fees are taken into account. Therefore, you might not be able to afford to buy that home because of the HOA. If you want to live in that particular neighborhood, you will need to find a less expensive home.

On average, using today's rates, what does a $100-a-month HOA fee do to your borrowing power? It means you will typically qualify for $18,000 less in your loan amount. If the property you want to buy has Mello-Roos or some other bond associated with it for $400 a month, this could lower your purchasing power by close to $60,000. A good loan originator will review all these items with you and prepare you accordingly.

Types of Loans

United States Department of Agriculture Home Loan Rural Program

The property you are interested in may qualify for a United States Department of Agriculture (USDA) loan. The USDA does more than just stamp your beef! They have 100% financing in their rural loan program. Using information on land use from the most recent available census, the USDA will make loans in areas

Ask About All Loan Possibilities

• Does the Property Qualify for 203K or USDA Loans?
• Does your loan originator do FHA (Federal Housing Administration) loans?
• How many lenders does the loan originator work with?
• What special loans are there for first-time buyers?

that the census deems rural. You may find in your own community that a few years ago, at the last census, what is now a fully developed neighborhood was a rural area. Does your loan officer know of USDA loans? Again, make sure that when you are interviewing loan originators you find someone who will consider your loan needs and look at all of the options available for you. This is what a professional and experienced originator should offer you as part of his/her services.

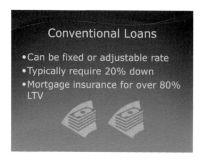

Federal Housing Administration 203K Streamline

The Federal Housing Administration (FHA) 203k Streamline is a great program when used correctly for the right property. The 203k program allows the consumer with only 3.5% down to appraise the property as if repair work required for occupancy and building code compliance were already complete for the purposes of securing financing. This allows repair costs to be funded in your first trust deed as part of one single loan. Through this program, you can help establish a better neighborhood by owner-occupying and raising the property value through repairs. A borrower who might pass on a home that is in need of up to approximately $30,000 in repairs may now purchase this home; select their own carpet, paint, and appliances; and finance all of these repairs into one first deed of trust.

Energy Efficient Loans

Energy efficiency is of great benefit if home buyers can take advantage of the FHA energy efficient mortgage ("EEM") program. If all qualified individuals availed themselves of this program, we could theoretically reduce greenhouse gases by up to 17% across the United States. When you buy a home and you get FHA financing, you automatically qualify for the EEM as long as you can demonstrate that there will be sufficient reductions in your electricity bill to justify the purchase of energy efficient appliances and simple retrofitting. You could actually use this program to purchase new windows or replace the old heating or air conditioning unit. All items that qualify a home as energy efficient can be applied to this loan. By doing so, you may put the cost of items toward your loan qualification. It is a great program to consider as an option.

If you mention the EEM program to your real estate professional, he or she may give you a blank stare. Many are not aware of this program. This is all about learning how to interview people you plan to work with. The average real estate agent has been in business for fewer than 10 years according to the National Association of REALTORS® website. Think of what the real estate industry has gone through in the past 6 to 10 years: loan programs such as stated income, stated assets, and subprime loans were the norm of the marketplace only a few years ago. Many practitioners, sadly, are woefully underprepared for today's market, and that is why consumers need to educate themselves and become more discerning. In fairness, the reader is encouraged to place much more emphasis on the ethical behavior of the professional than complete product knowledge. An ethical professionals can always find an answer for you.

Veterans Loans

Veterans Administration (VA) loans can be a great opportunity for veterans or members of our armed forces. VA loans provide up to 100% financing. They require a certificate of eligibility and very similar underwriting criteria to FHA loans.

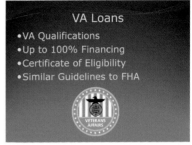

California Housing Finance Authority

The California Housing Finance Authority ("CalHFA") is a great resource for homebuyers in our state. Conventional loans typically require 20% down. The CalHFA has financing options for low- to moderate-income first-time homebuyers. They offer low interest rates, down payment assistance, and up to 100% financing. The most common program requires 3% down, although there are some programs where no down payment is required. The tradeoff is that you will pay a significant mortgage insurance premium (MIP) for no-down-payment financing options.

Special Programs for Teachers

CalHFA has a special program for teachers who work in challenged schools, using the school's Academic Performance Index (API) scores as developed and reported by the California Department of Education. Schools with an API score of 5 or lower often have trouble keeping teachers. This turnover further hurts students at these schools. CalHFA provides a financial incentive to teachers that will actually commit to teach in a low-API school for three years or more by giving those borrowers additional incentives. If you are a schoolteacher, or work at one of these schools, please make sure to investigate this program.

FHA Loans (Federal Housing Administration)

Traditional private lenders have tightened their lending practices, and it has become harder and harder to get a traditional bank loan. The Federal Housing Administration (FHA) has stepped in to make up some of that gap by providing borrowers with a 3.5% down and "make sense" underwriting guidelines. Underwriters look carefully to see if the loans make sense, if they are truly affordable for the buyer. This is probably one of the greatest loan programs out there, and it is why this program has exploded in growth. Your 3.5% down payment can be all gifts. A little-known fact is that the gift can also come

? Ask the Expert

Question: If you do not have good established credit but have lots in savings, is that beneficial for acquiring a loan?

Answer: No. If you do not have credit, it tells a lender that you may not know how to manage your finances well enough to make regular monthly payments to pay off a loan. On a smaller scale, the lender wants to see that you can have at least four credit cards upon which you borrow and pay back. If you have only two credit card or trade lines. FHA guidelines allow for "alternative credit." Examples of alternative credit include: car insurance paid on time every single month, cell phone payments made every single month, or any other type of regular installment debt. Be sure and ask your loan originator upfront if their company has what is commonly referred to as "investor overlays" that can be more restrictive than standard FHA guidelines.

from your employer, as long as your employer is not going to ask you to pay it back. Documentation of this gift is critical and your loan professional should be very familiar with what a borrower and the donor must provide. It has to be clearly documented that the money is truly a gift and not a loan.

Whether you seek conventional or government financing for your home purchase, be sure to take your time and choose a loan professional that will not make you feel rushed or embarrassed for asking questions. You have many options. Based on your own unique set of circumstances, you should do what is in your long-term best interest, not just what is easy at the moment.

Reverse Mortgages

Reverse mortgages are typically used by people who already own their homes, and meet the age requirement of 62 years or older. However, few know that this important senior benefit from HUD can be used for home purchase, too. The key underwriting guidelines are the condition of the property and a very low loan-to-value ratio. In other words, to qualify for this, you must own your home without a loan at all, or owe very little compared to the value of the home. Reverse mortgages allow you to remain in your residence with no monthly mortgage payment. The mortgage can be designed to supplement your fixed income to cover daily expenses. It does not subject you to additional income tax. It does require counseling to ensure that you are well-informed on how the loan works prior to making a decision. You do need to take into consideration and learn if applying for a reverse mortgage affects you in other financial areas. It can affect your need-based government assistance qualification. Many predatory lenders have put people in destructive reverse mortgages, so be sure to be well informed and ask many questions before pursuing this kind of loan.

Reverse mortgages have received a lot of press in the past few years. Some press has been favorable and some not. It is simply another financial vehicle that should be fully explained to determine if the extra income received on a monthly basis is worth any sacrifices that must be made.

Government Assistance Programs

There is a wide variety of government assistance programs out there, and the requirements change often and vary from county to county and city to city. There are programs for down payment assistance and closing costs. Programs are available from the federal, state, and local municipalities. Talk to your real estate professionals, but do not just take their word for it. If you are interested in government assistance programs, be sure to work with an agent that has experience in this area. You can also research this online.

Government Assistance
- Down payment
- Closing costs
- Mortgage credit certificate
- Tax credits
  - Energy efficiency tax credit
  - First-time home buyer
- Ask your county or city about special programs tailored for homebuyers or owners

Call your county and city agencies and ask what first-time homebuyer assistance programs are available. Inquire if the programs are still active and have funds to distribute. There are generally up to four programs available. Often times they will also have a list of professionals, both agents and loan officers, that are "certified" and approved to work with the agency. This approval means that the professional have received training on how to work with the agency to submit the required documentation.

Look up your local economic development agency, redevelopment agency, and housing department to see what programs are available. Ask your county or city about special programs tailored for homebuyers and homeowners. Cities and counties have redevelopment agencies and counties have economic development agencies. A simple explanation is that for local agencies to retrieve property tax monies back from Sacramento, they must pledge to set aside 20% for low- and moderate-income families. You may visit www.hud.gov and search "HUD Median Income" to determine what the income restrictions are for your given area.

Sometimes it can be hard to find these homebuyer assistance programs, so you may have to make several phone calls. Stick with it, because it is worth it if it helps you get into your home.

Mortgage Credit Certificate

You always want to find out if you can qualify for the mortgage credit certificate (MCC). It converts some of your mortgage interest deduction into a direct credit on your taxes, giving you much greater tax savings. This will help you qualify for more home and also help you receive the tax benefits of homeownership immediately. Almost every county has an MCC program. You need to qualify for the MCC credit during escrow, when you are in the process of getting your loan. If you wait until your purchase is completed, it is too late. Qualifying for the program is based on earning up to 120% of the local median income according to the HUD (Department of Housing and Urban Development).

• Impound Accounts for Property Taxes and Fire Insurance

Impound accounts are most often required when a borrower has a down payment of less than 20%. In this case, the lender collects extra money for taxes and property insurance in addition to the money toward principal and interest, and rolls it all together into your loan payment. Essentially, you make one payment to the lender. The lender holds the collected money in an impound account and pays it out when it is due, twice a year for taxes and once a year for your insurance. Borrowers can run into big problems if their impound account is not set up correctly. Ensure that all the taxes on the property are calculated correctly. Ask your real estate agent to help you verify this and confirm the amounts by checking with the tax collector's office. Make sure that any Mello-Roos or parcel taxes have been included. Review your tax bill to determine that you are taxed correctly on the assessed value of the house.

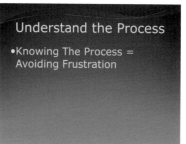

Protect Yourself

- An Impound Account is where taxes and insurance are collected as part of your monthly payment
- The lender holds the collected money and pays for taxes and insurance when required

- Make sure your impound account is set up properly

• Summary

There is a lot more about borrowing than most people who have already bought a home realize. What was working a year or two ago is not working today. Make sure you secure a loan you can afford by being clear with your lender about all your expenses, and what you can afford for a down payment, closing costs, and a monthly payment. This will be easy to do if you have a budget. Be sure to find professionals with your best interest in mind to help you through this process.

Understand the Process

- Knowing The Process = Avoiding Frustration

Module 3: Buying

Which kind of buyer do you want to be? One is the "typical buyer," who tells their agent they would like to buy a $300,000 home, when they really qualify for $250,000. Another is the "conservative buyer," who knows the loan he can qualify for and afford and, has considered his own unique budget based on careful planning and review. You have taken the time to come to this class and learn about borrowing. You understand your budget, have been saving for years, and can easily document those savings. You say to your real estate agent and lender, "I qualify for a $375,000 home, but I only want to buy a $325,000 home. You have researched programs and know that you want to take advantage of the local first-time homebuyer down payment program. Clearly, this second type of buyer is the one you wish to be. This is all about setting yourself up for success.

Buying
Financial Literacy: Module 3
From Financial Sense
to White Picket Fence

Module 3: Buying
Student Learning Outcomes
Students will be able to:
• Explain the meaning of a contract/offer to purchase as a legal document.
• List common buyer expenses incurred in escrow
• State approximate amounts needed for a down payment and closing costs for purchase of a nearby home.
• Describe what an escrow calendar is.

• Read the Documents Before Signing

No matter what anyone says, you have the right and responsibility to read everything you sign. Do not let anyone talk you into signing documents without reading them. Legal documents can have serious negative impacts on you now and in the future. Most people want to be nice. They do not want to make the escrow officer or the real estate agent wait while they read. But this is the time to look out for yourself! This is your future at stake, not theirs. It is their job to make sure you understand what you are signing. Part of this is allowing you the time necessary to read the documents."

• More Reasons to Interview Your Professionals

When you interview professionals, you are looking for someone who wants your business—not just for this transaction, but also for a lifetime of referrals. This is a relationship, often an emotional one, because you are dealing with somebody who is going to help place you and your family into a home. You want someone who practices 100% accountability, someone you can trust. If you go back to your agent with a problem after the sale has closed, you want to know that you are working with someone who will help you, even if the commission has been paid. Make sure you as a consumer hire the right professionals and then rely on them.

All individuals representing buyers and sellers in real estate transactions must be licensed as a salesperson or broker by the State of California Department of Real Estate. Salespersons must affiliate their license with a broker in order to act as an agent. In addition, many licensees take an additional step and join a professional real estate organization. There are many from which to choose. All aspire to a code of ethics that encourages the highest level of fiduciary responsibility to their clients and community. The California Association of REALTORS® (CAR®) with members identified as REALTORS®.

Second only in longevity in California is The National Association of Real Estate Brokers® (NAREB) with members identified as Realtists®. Additional professional organizations notably include: The National Association of Hispanic Real Estate Professionals (NAHREP), the Chinese American Real Estate Association (CAREA), and the Filipino American Real Estate Professional Association (FAREPA).

When you are on a plane and you hit turbulence, how many of you unfasten your seatbelts, run up to the cabin, bang on the door and say, "Let me inside there to see what is going on!" You would be arrested! Allow the captain, whether that is your agent or your loan officer, to handle the little emergencies. Let them put out the small fires; let them be your firefighter. Neither loan process nor escrow goes perfectly. Find somebody you can trust and then sit down and fasten your seatbelt, and hang on because there is going to be turbulence in the process of buying a home. This is why it is so important to interview professionals and ensure that you are working with people you can trust.

• Fiduciary Responsibility

Both your loan originator and your real estate agent have a fiduciary responsibility to you. In very simple terms, fiduciary responsibility is putting a client's interest above your own. It means that your loan originator and your real estate agent are legally required to work for your financial best interest, not theirs. Now that sounds very simple, but how does it translate to real life? If you are looking in a particular neighborhood for a particular model home, your agent may find one that is a bank foreclosure resale with a price way below market value. The agent knows that the property is a great deal and if the agent was to buy this property, she or he could turn it around and make an extra $5,000-$10,000 if they do not tell you about this particular property. But if this is a property that they think you would be interested in, they are required to tell you about it. Do they have your best interest at heart? Not if they do not tell you about the property. That is a violation of the business and professions code and that behavior can cause them problems. Fiduciary responsibility is making sure that you as a professional always put your clients' interests above your own; professional ethics and fiduciary responsibility are extremely crucial.

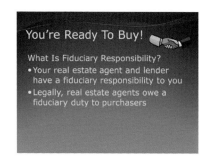

? Ask the Expert

Question: What do you do if you have not received a copy of your deed of trust?

Answer: Your agent can help you get a copy of your deed of trust. Agents have relationships with title companies and can get documents from them with ease. A good agent is a great document-keeper, among many other things. In order for agents to get their commission check, their broker and their errors and omissions insurance carrier will both require that they have a complete file on your transaction. You can ask your agent to give you a closing package that has copies of all documentation in it. They should keep a copy of this

Questions?

information in a secure location in case it is ever needed. When you go to buy again, several years down the road, there is nothing more appealing than working with an agent who already has all your records right there, ready at a moment's notice.

Documentation is also vital for people who are losing their homes. If you are losing your home today, the more you can show that you have done everything possible to help the lender get the most money possible for that property, the more it will actually help you buy again three years down the road. According to FHA guidelines, if you can prove that your foreclosure was beyond your ability to control and you can document your hardship, after three years of time you can actually buy again. Even foreclosure is not the end of the world.

● Hire Licensed AND Ethical Professionals

It is best to engage an agent who you know is ethical and puts the client's interests above his or her own, even if that agent has been in the business for just an hour. But you must check an agent's license status to ensure his or her license is current and that there have not been any complaints filed against them. You can look up their license status online at the California Department of Real Estate website, www.ca.dre.gov, by name or by license number. Look up any real estate professional you plan to work with. If you look them up and you see complaints or an expired license, or if you cannot find them listed at all, do not work with that person. Before you engage a professional, make sure you check them out.

Now, if you expect 100% accountability from your professionals, you also need to follow that guideline. You need to tell your professionals what you expect from them, and put it in writing. Then it is up to you to inspect their work. You need to follow up. Ultimately, this is your house and your deal, so you have to be willing to inspect the work done by your professionals. This means reading all your loan documentation before you sign. It means asking questions when you do not understand something and not letting it go because you are in a hurry. Put your expectations in writing and have the people you work with sign it. Be willing to do the same for any professionals that set reasonable expectations for you. Be assertive if you must, but please do not allow yourself to feel overly pressured.

• Identifying Expectations

Some real estate professionals in moments of frustration have used the expression, "buyers are liars." What they mean by this is that buyers rarely really want what they say they want. Buyers are not liars, but often professionals do not know how to set proper expectations or glean information from the buyer to determine what he or she truly wants. Sometimes buyers are confused. You may think that you want a particular home in a particular neighborhood, so you tell the agent to find you this particular home in this neighborhood. Then you turn around and buy an adorable, but completely different kind of home in another neighborhood and the agent is frustrated because she or he invested time and energy to show you the properties you said you wanted to see and then bought something completely different, using an agent you just met. Real estate agents and buyers need to get together and express in writing what they want out of that relationship and then be willing to sign off on it.

• A Fun Exercise Before Shopping For Your Home

Marcia and Brad are a couple looking to purchase a home. Marcia thinks they are going to buy a particular type of home in her head and Brad is thinking that there is no way they are going to buy that particular type of home. With married couples or more than one buyer, often one party will get started and do the research upfront and then the other party will come in behind, leaving the poor real estate agent to start all over again because the two never agreed on what they wanted in the first place.

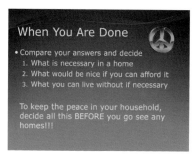

Save Time and Energy

Know what you are looking for before you go out looking.

- All the decision makers should participate in the decision-making process
- Grab two pieces of paper
- Write down the style and type of home you are looking for plus features (pool, BBQ?)
- Then mark which features you cannot live without on a scale of 1 to 5

When You Are Done

- Compare your answers and decide
  1. What is necessary in a home
  2. What would be nice if you can afford it
  3. What you can live without if necessary

To keep the peace in your household, decide all this BEFORE you go see any homes!!!

When two people are buying a home together, they should do the following exercise before looking at any houses. If their children are old enough to have an opinion, they should consider having them participate as well. Without looking at anyone else's paper, everyone doing the exercise writes down the features that she or he is looking for in a home. Do not skip this exercise because it is too simple! The lists will likely be very different. Now, without sharing anything on the list, rate each item on a scale of 1 to 5, based on how important it is that the home you buy has this feature. A score of "5" indicates that you would eliminate the property from consideration altogether if it does not have this feature. Then, have a discussion and decide together what you require in a home, what would be nice if you could get, and what you do not need or want. You will find that most of the time the lists do not match but you can come to an agreement on your home search if you work at it. Once you know what you want, you can give directional steps in writing to your practitioner to utilize that relationship to everybody's benefit.

Buyers are not liars, they are just emotional. A professional will assist the buyer in truly understanding what all of the buying parties actually want in their next home and then guide them

❓ Ask the Expert

Question: As an investor, is it a good idea to buy a foreclosed home?

Answer: It depends. The answer rests with whether the asking price is at or above market value. At the end of the day, it matters not whether a home is a typical sale or a foreclosed property as long the value is confirmed and protections are in place.

Investors are often willing to pay a premium because current rents provide a positive cash flow. Therefore, investors are buying not only short sales but also REOs (bank-owned properties) at auctions. Fannie Mae and Freddie Mac conduct auctions as well, often exclusively for first-time homebuyers with no investors allowed.

towards a successful purchase. It may be a good idea to do this exercise even before you meet a real estate agent. Ensure your thoughts and desires are clear and considered before you interact with a professional.

• California Residential Purchase Agreement and Escrow Instructions

When you make an offer on a property and your offer is accepted, you are in a legally binding contract. You need to read the contract in full before you make an offer. The contract is designed to protect you, but you have to know what you are promising. The contracts used in the purchase of your property

Bring on the Paperwork!

- This is the largest purchase most people will make
- Your offer to purchase a property is a LEGAL CONTRACT
- To protect yourself, you MUST READ the contract and fine print
- The contract is designed to protect you
- If English is your second language, demand a neutral interpreter

will most likely be those created by the California Association of REAL-TORS® which has a team of attorneys that review and create the paperwork that you will be signing. A purchase agreement, signed by both buyer and seller, is a contractual obligation. You have rights but you also have responsibilities and potential liability. The first page of the contract is all about the financing, including a receipt for a deposit on the property. If you sign this, it means you are going to follow through and buy this property as long as the terms you requested are adhered.

• Agency Disclosure

There are many disclosures involved in California real estate transactions. Again, these are generally created to protect the buyer. Read the disclosures and ask questions if you need to. One required disclosure is regarding real estate relationships. This document officially records which agent is representing the buyers' interests and which is representing the sellers' interests. Real estate agents can either represent the buyer exclusively or the seller exclusively, and in California they are allowed to represent both. This is called a dual agency. That means one agent is representing the best interests of both the buyer and the seller in the same deal. Some people question how one agent can represent the conflicting interests of both sides in a purchase of a home, but it is legal in California as long as the agent discloses that fact to both parties. You are not required to work with someone who wants dual agency. You can always go and find another agent before you make the offer. If you have any concern about whether or not the agent is acting as a dual agent or has your best interest at heart, just stop the process. You can still stop at that point, even in escrow, and say you are no longer comfortable with the dual agency role. The California Association of REALTORS® and others believe this point so important that their current contract places this issue on the first page of the document along with the financing details.

• Real Estate Transfer Disclosure Statement

The Transfer Disclosure Statement (TDS) is another important disclosure form. This is a statement from the seller disclosing to the buyer significant information about the property. It is a way for the buyer to hold the seller accountable. For example, you may move into a home in the summer and not realize until the first rainy season hits that there are drainage issues on the property. Some of the stuff in your garage is damaged because water collected on the outside of the garage and flowed under the garage door. A contractor inspects the garage and can see this has been an ongoing problem. Then you realize that the sellers rearranged a little wall to hide the problem, and you realize they had knowledge of this situation. The sellers had "constructive knowledge" that this was a problem. You can go back to the Transfer Disclosure Statement to see if they actually disclosed this information. If they did not you have a potential civil lawsuit. This of course is not to be construed as legal advice, but this underscores just how important this particular form can be.

• Home Warranty

You want to get a home warranty, which will cover expenses for a $50-$100 deductible on most required repairs. The home warranty can be renewed each year after you buy it, but make sure that you get the home warranty before you close escrow. It is inexpensive insurance for what it can save you. The seller may even elect to pay for the policy because she or he wants to avoid any liability. Home warranties are popular with both buyers and sellers as components in homes can work without any challenges for years and can fail shortly after a buyer takes possession. A home warranty policy allows the buyer to get this unexpected appliance failure repaired with little out-of-pocket. The seller avoids accusations by a potentially frustrated buyer claiming the seller knew the component was about to fail.

• If English Is Your Second Language, Find a Neutral Interpreter

If English is your second language, demand a neutral interpreter, even if it is at your own expense. You must be able to understand what you are signing. The homebuying process and all the legal documents you have to sign are complex and use a lot of legal language. They can be tricky even for native speakers of English to understand. For a few hundred dollars, you can find somebody that will interpret so that you do not sign something you do not understand. Many homebuyers have claimed that they were given false information by an unscrupulous real estate professionals and they did not understand what they were signing. They then sign something very different from their original expectations. Some of these individuals accepted loans that did not really fit their financial circumstances and have now lost those homes. If you are buying a home and do not understand the language, do not sign the paperwork. A professional interpreter may be the best few hundred dollars you will spend to avoid potentially tens of thousands of damages.

• Escrow Process

Escrow is the period between when an offer is accepted and when the documents are signed and the new ownership is officially recorded. In California, a neutral third party handles escrows. Neutral means that the escrow company cannot favor the buyer or the seller, and the escrow agent has a fiduciary responsibility to both parties. The escrow officer will handle funds and loan documents, and will issue title insurance. Your lender may require title insurance prior to releasing funds for the loan to purchase.

> **What's an Escrow?**
>
> • Independent, neutral third party
> • Responsible for holding and transferring funds between the buyer, seller and lenders
> • General home inspection
> • Pest inspection
> • Home warranty

Other activities that occur during escrow include various professional inspections, the appraisal, identification of an insurance agent and policy for the home, finalization of the loan, and completion of repairs required by the lender.

There are three California agencies regulating the escrow industry: the Department of Real Estate, the Department of Corporations, and the Department of Insurance. The Department of Insurance covers the escrows as they relate to title insurance. The Department of Corporations governs the independent escrow companies that can do business with anybody. Finally, the Department of Real Estate regulates escrows where a real estate broker's license is involved in every step of the sales transaction, such as in cases of a real estate broker who has an escrow department. You should

? Ask the Expert

Question: How long will interest rates remain low? In addition, will property values continue to drop and for how long?

Answer: Unfortunately, I think we are going to see values further depress in certain markets. Our highest-risk markets are known as the "sunshine" states. This is where the greatest appreciation occurred and where many experts believe we need to see more depreciation before we return to normal appreciation. Only one-third of the foreclosed inventory is actually on the market right now. As of September 2010, Fannie Mae reported that for every home sold they are taking back one and a third more. Many experts forecast that 2011 will have slightly higher unemployment than 2010, and that the unemployment rate and negative equity will peak this year. We Californians have some mounting challenges. Many experts predict that we will just "bounce along the bottom" for a while. Will we have a double-dip recession? According to Allen Greenspan, former Chairman of the Federal Reserve Board, there is a 50/50 chance that this will happen. Housing is one-sixth of our economy and housing starts are not going to pull us out of this recession as they have in the past. The rebounding of the economy is going to be a long, long process.

I think rates will stay down low as well. Whatever the upcoming financial cycle is, do not fall into the same traps as the people who are now losing their homes. You can always say no and borrow less. Interest rates will probably start to increase the minute employment stabilizes and will shoot up 100 to 200 basis points (1% or 2% higher) than they are now. This is an opinion based on numerous economists' observations.

ask your practitioners whether the Department of Insurance, Department of Corporations or the Department of Real Estate regulate the referred escrow company.

• Title Insurance

Your lender will require that you buy title insurance to protect their interest and ensure that the security instrument, the deed, remains in a first lien position. The seller buys title insurance to protect the buyer and ensure full disclosure of all liens, easements or other encumbrances prior to closing escrow. Each policy covers different aspects of title, so make sure to ask questions so you understand the coverage. The escrow company will also disclose restrictions on title, easements, or restrictions on rights of use by providing title insurance information to both the buyer and the seller. An easement grants someone else permission to use your property. For example, let us say your public utility has a particular easement that covers your back yard. When you looked at the home, you decided the backyard was the perfect place for a pool. When you go to build a pool after you buy the property, you find out that you should have read the title report because it clearly disclosed that there was an easement in favor of the utility company granting use of the yard, and now you cannot build a pool in the desired location, or at all. You will receive a preliminary title report that discloses this kind of information within days of having your offer accepted and opening escrow. Ask your real estate agent or the escrow officer to go over it with you. It is a half-hour process and well worth the time.

Question: There once was a "cooling-off period" after signing a loan document— a review period. Does that still exist?

Answer: Yes, it does. You have a three-day cooling-off period, called a right of rescission, thanks to the Truth in Lending Act of 1968. The right of rescission means you can cancel the loan within that three-day period. As a borrower, you may still be liable for upholding your end of the Residential Purchase Agreement. You can read about the right of rescission in the Real Estate Settlement Procedures Act, RESPA, Title 12, section 2605e, which addresses the lender's responsibilities and your rights.

Trust Deeds

The bank wants to know that if they lend you money, the loan is in first position, meaning that if something goes wrong with the loan, that lender will be paid back first. People talk about first trust deeds, second trust deeds and third trust deeds. What most people call a mortgage in California is actually a trust deed. A mortgage or loan to a borrower is secured by deed of trust recorded as a lien against the subject property. Whether something is in first, second or third position depends on what order it is recorded at the county recorder's office. Lenders want to know that if something happens that "clouds" the title of the property, the title insurance company is going to pay them off completely, or fix the problem.

Home Inspection

You should have a physical inspection, or "contractor's inspection," done on the property once your offer has been accepted. Remember, you specified that you would perform this inspection within a number of days after the offer was accepted. If you fail to perform this critical step per the contract, you will lose you right to do so. A licensed inspector walks through the property and checks for all visible problems or flaws. An inspector would report water stains on the floor joists, for example, as an indi-

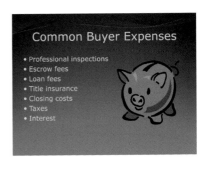

Common Buyer Expenses

- Professional inspections
- Escrow fees
- Loan fees
- Title insurance
- Closing costs
- Taxes
- Interest

cation of possible leaking or water problems. The inspector would not be able to detect a wiring problem hidden in the wall, however; their report is based only upon what they can physically see. Paying for these inspectors is part of the buyer's expense during escrow, and home inspections usually cost anywhere from $200 to $400, but can be more for larger properties. It is well worth the money to have this inspection done, because not everything will show up on the Transfer Disclosure Statement. The inspector will give you a detailed report of everything discovered about the property, but he or she may not do any of the repair work noted in the report.

The reports are very detailed and often quite lengthy, and can be very intimidating to read through. You may read in an inspector's report that there is a cracked foundation, illegal wiring, and leaking plumbing in the home you wish to buy. You may wonder if you really want this house after all, because there appears to be so much to fix. If you go to your agent with a whole litany of things you want fixed, things could become contentious between the homebuyer and the home seller, requiring the agents have to get involved and a lot of re-negotiating to take place. How can you avoid this situation? It is possible that some of the problems are not as bad as they sound on paper. The best thing to do is to accompany the inspector on his or her walkthrough of the property. He or she will explain everything that is going to be in the report and you will also be able to ask the inspector's opinion as a contractor, which you cannot get in the report. Then, when you get the 35-page report, you will understand how to interpret it and will have the perspective to make the correct decision.

• Know Your Rights in an "As Is" Sale

Many people misunderstand what it means to sell "as is." Even if you buy a home "as is," you still have rights. "As is" really means that you are buying the property in its current condition. The sellers still have to fill out a Transfer Disclosure Statement, and disclose everything they know is wrong with the property. Completion of this form is mandated for any owner-occupied home

of one to four units. You can and should have a physical inspection on an "as is" sale, because the lender may require some repairs to be done. After the physical inspection, you can still go back and demand certain repairs, or negotiate a lower price. Home warranty policies exclude pre-existing conditions, but you still want to have a home warranty for an "as is" property as standard practice. It is just the prudent thing to do.

• Know Your Neighborhood

Take a trip down to your city or county government offices to find out what is happening in the neighborhood around your prospective property. If there is a vacant field across the street from the home you are buying, you will want to know what that property is zoned for, and when development might occur. If you ask your real estate agent about the empty lot and they

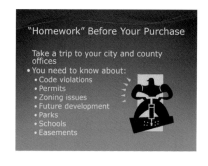

inform you that it is zoned residential and that eventually there will be homes there, you could take that agent's word, move in, and six months later the owners of the lot might start building a large church that operates a five-day-a-week school that brings traffic to your street. Your first impulse may be to sue your agent. However, if you had gone down to city hall, you would have found that this project has been an item of discussion for the last twelve months and that while it is true that the property was zoned for residential development, the owners were successful in their request for a Conditional Use Permit. You want to know about things like this BEFORE closing escrow. So take a field trip to your local government offices and find out what is happening in and around the neighborhood that could affect your home-buying decision. You also want to find out about nearby code violations, permits, and zoning issues, future developments, parks, schools, easements, or other matters that could affect your property. All of this information is fully disclosed and available at city hall.

• Make an Escrow Calendar

Timing is everything. When you sign the Residential Purchase Agreement, you promise to fulfill specific duties by specific dates. How do you make sure you do not miss something by mistake? Create an escrow calendar. Start with the projected date of the close of escrow, and work backwards. A good real estate professional will keep you on target with this, but it is your responsibility too. In the current lending environment, it is possible the banks or lenders will have trouble keeping to the timeline, especially if you are dealing with a short sale or foreclosure sale. Regardless, you will need to uphold your end of the bargain.

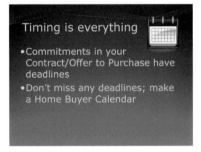

Work backwards from the date you want to get your keys and get into the home. Ask the escrow officer and the lender which date they need to fund your loan by, so that you can get the keys when you want them. What does it mean for your loan to be funded? The funded loan payment is routed through the Federal Reserve Bank in San Francisco. In this manner, large amounts of money moving through the banking system are tracked. The money from there goes to the title company, which then pays off the seller's loans and other debts on the property because they are the ones insuring it for clear and unencumbered title. The title company receives confirmation of funding and electronically records the grant deed in most California counties. Once this task is complete, we have what is referred to as confirmation of recording along with the confirmation of funding. The title insurance company then takes the remaining proceeds and wires them to the escrow company, which pays the commissions and any remaining costs. Ultimately, the escrow company will refund you whatever money is over the balance. Buyers always have a little bit of money left over because escrow companies make sure they have more than enough money to cover all the down payment, closing costs and other miscellaneous costs associated with your home purchase. You will receive a refund for any overage you paid.

• How Long Does it Take to Fund the Loan?

How long does this process typically take? It takes at least two days to fund a loan. If you are talking about the end of the month, the shifting around of funds could cause a four- to six-hour delay.

Question: In your opinion, is this the right time to invest in a home?

Answer: Yes. There has never been a better time than today. If you buy today and values go down 10% on a $250,000 purchase, your property goes down $25,000 as a paper loss. You only feel that loss if you sell. If you are an investor prepared to buy and hold a property for many years, you are considering positive cash flow and long-term rate of return on your investment rather than short-term gain by buying and flipping the home for a quick profit. You want to borrow money now because today's low interest rates will offset a near-term drop in value. Investing in real estate is extremely competitive and one should not enter into this arena without careful planning. With this said, the cost of money is artificially low and if you are able to take advantage of this opportunity, you should. We will likely not see this type of market again in our lifetime.

This means the recording of the new deed will likely be deferred to the next day, which could mean the difference between new homeowners receiving their keys on a Friday versus a Monday. Agents often do not consider this delay as this is not their area of expertise. If you want your keys by Friday, your loan needs to fund first thing Wednesday morning to be safe. Anything after that is a gamble because you are relying on other people. On your escrow calendar, you need to take out weekends, and add in extra time in case somebody calls in sick to work. After factoring these things in, you have a very small window of time to get everything done that you need to do. You have written down your expectations with your loan originator and your real estate agent. Do not forget to follow up. It is a good idea is to call each of them every Monday morning and ask them to go through what is supposed to be happening with your purchase during the week. Find out if you are on target. Make sure anything important is in writing, because if it is not in writing, it just does not exist. Remember to document everything. Read the seller's disclosure and both agents' inspections.

> ### If It's Not In Writing, It Doesn't Exist!
> - Get everything in writing to avoid financial peril
> - If you aren't good at understanding contracts, ask your agent to explain
> - Read the sellers' and agents' inspections

Confirm with your loan professional that everything promised in terms of interest rate, fees, down payment, and other costs has remained the same. If you have already looked at the paperwork and confirmed, you can feel comfortable signing. When your loan closes, you will get a copy of the settlement, which is called the HUD- 1 form. You will get an estimated one of these forms earlier in the escrow process, but when you close escrow, you will get the final version. It is a very good idea to ask to review the most up-to-date HUD-1 and compare it to your good faith estimate immediately prior to going in to sign all of your loan documents. There should be very few if any discrepancies. In fact, for most items, there is a less-than-10% allowed variance. Anything greater must be absorbed by the issuer of the original good faith estimate.

The final HUD-1 is the rule of law. Check it over carefully and ask your questions prior to closing. When reading and signing closing documents, be sure to read the promissory note carefully. The promissory note is the contract between you and the lender on how you are going to pay back

? Ask the Expert

Question: Can you buy a foreclosed home with a loan or do you have to pay all cash?

Answer: No, the home does not have to be purchased with cash. If you are buying a home that has been foreclosed upon, you will need to qualify for a loan and the lenders will base the decision on the appraised value of the home and your financial qualifications. There are two approvals that need to happen for the purchase to succeed.

One is approval of you, the borrower. The other is approval by the bank of the property. Qualifications for loan were once based heavily on the property because values were increasing so fast. Lenders were focused on assessing the property instead of assessing the borrower. Today, we know property values will either go down or remain relatively flat for some time to come, so lenders are more focused on assessing the borrower.

the money that you are borrowing. It describes not only your rights, but the lender's rights as well. Did you know that most promissory notes allow a lender to physically inspect their asset? There are many nuances in the note that are important for you to understand, as this is a large legal contract and one that you will be making payments on for a very long time.

• Making Payments and What Happens When You Do Not Make Them

Congratulations! You are now a homeowner, with regular monthly payments. Let us look at an example with the Bank of Super Duper Trust. Chad has taken out a loan for $200,000 to buy a home, and the payment is due on the first of each month. When is the payment late? To get this right, you need to think like the bank. If a payment is due on the first, it is late on the second. You and the bank agreed to abide by many things as detailed contractually in the promissory note. This includes, but is not limited to, the timing of payments made and received.

Let us assume for a moment that poor Chad has run into some difficulty. Like many, he failed to take this course and purchased a home that was slightly above his means. In addition, he failed to budget properly in order to know what he truly could afford long-term. Loans usually have a 10- to 15-day grace period before borrowers are assessed a penalty. However, if the lender receives Chad's payment on the 16th of that month, there is a late payment and penalty assessed as agreed in writing in the promissory note. If his payment is not received by the first of the following month, he is now 30 days late and the bank can report that late payment to the credit bureaus and ruin his credit. Thank you, Bank of Super Duper Trust! Now Chad has a late mark on his mortgage credit, which is very injurious.

If Chad is unable to make his payments, late on his second payment, or two months behind, the bank can take a number of actions. It can do nothing. In fact, this is occurring more and more at the time of this writing due to the overwhelming number of homeowners who are falling behind. Eventually the bank will do something, but at this particular moment, it may simply be too busy dealing with other borrowers who are failing to make their monthly payments. It may decide to sue the borrower in court and foreclose using a process normally referred to as the Judicial Foreclosure Process. This particular path is rarely taken by the lender, as it can be long, costly, and extends the right of redemption for up to twelve months after the process is complete. Almost all of the time, the lender will follow a procedure commonly referred to as the Non-Judicial Foreclosure Process, which in California is described in California Real Estate Fraud Report, California Civil Code, Sections 2924–2945.

The first step of the non-judicial foreclosure process is for the Bank of Super Duper Trust to file a notice of default against Chad. He could actually be behind in payments for over a year, but not be in foreclosure until this notice is filed. Once the notice of default is recorded at the county recorder's office, Chad has 90 days to "redeem" the note and bring the loan current. If Chad does this, the lender must adhere to the terms of the original note. This redemption period is designed to allow a borrower to financially recover by borrowing from family members or finding other means to "cure" their delinquent payments.

If Chad is unable to do that and goes another three months without making a payment, the next step in the non-judicial foreclosure process is a notice of trustee sale, or NOT. Now Chad only has 21 more days before the bank will sell the home at a public auction, and only 15 days to bring his loan current in this final redemption period. Once it is within five days of the actual sale date, the banks can demand loan pay-off in full instead of being bound by the original terms of the loan. Read your promissory note to see if your lender has included this provision. Always get a copy in advance of the entire set of documents that you will be signing at closing if possible to make sure you take a careful look at this. To avoid this entire process, pay your mortgage payments on time and always buy well within your means.

• Ready, Set, Time to Close Escrow

Are the funds for your down payment and closing costs verified and ready as required by your preliminary approval? If so, you may close escrow. You cannot just walk in on the day you sign documents and hand over a check. The funds you bring in must be the exact funds you verified through the loan approval process and documented as such. Not being able to verify funds to close

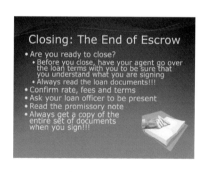

is the number one reason why escrows close late. One cannot demonstrate "proof of funds" by providing bank statements from one bank and then wire money from another bank. All money must be easily tracked through financial institutions. Money saved under the mattress or in a piggy bank will not do until they have been seasoned in a bank. Your funds have to be certified funds, or wire transferred with sufficient time to clear escrow before closing. Remember to factor in any holidays that may affect the time it takes for your money to transfer.

• Things to Remember Before Closing

Have you chosen a proper homeowners insurance policy to cover damage in the case of hazard, flood, earthquake or other situations? There are many different types of insurance. Make sure that you are properly insured; do not just use a friend's insurance agent as an afterthought. Take the time to make sure you have an agent that you feel comfortable with and the proper insurance; go over your options early in the process of looking for a home. Homeowners insurance costs can vary based on a number of factors. Talk with your insurance agent and make sure you budget accurately for the proper amount of insurance and a deductible that is affordable for you.

Other Things to Have Ready

- Are your funds to close in escrow, or accessible?
- Are the funds properly documented?
- Have you made arrangements for homeowners' insurance before close of escrow?
  - Fire, hazard, flood, earthquake
- Don't forget the final walkthrough

Do not forget to take the final walkthrough that you are allowed before the close of escrow. The purpose of this walkthrough is to confirm that the property is still in the same condition that it was in when your offer was made, or that required repairs have been completed. It is the time to check and confirm the sellers have not removed any items included in the sale. This is not the time to start renegotiating

Often, during the process of the transaction, buyers and sellers have offended each other to a certain extent. We witness over and over again how both parties will wish to "take a stand" at the last minute over what are typically very trivial issues as viewed in retrospect. A good thought to consider is that we should not allow the negative actions of others to dictate our own. Focus on the big picture and remind yourself that if the seller takes an extra day to move, as frustrating as this may be and as legally right as you may be to make demands, it may be better for you and your family to focus on the years of enjoyment this home will bring to you in the future rather than on the one extra day that you have to wait before moving in.

Module 4: Beyond

Congratulations, you are now a homeowner! You have a personal and financial stake in your home and your community. In this section, we will cover things you need to do to preserve and grow your financial stake in your home, and to be the new example of an active homeowner in your community.

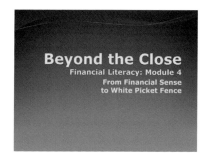

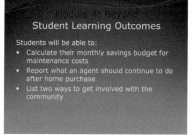

• Keep a Maintenance Budget

Now that you own your home, you need to maintain it. If something breaks, you are the one that must deal with it and pay for it. Repairs and maintenance are a fact with all properties, even new ones. You can and must expect repairs to be needed and need to budget for them accordingly. Having money saved and ready for repairs will also give you peace of mind so that you are not always worrying about how you will pay for the next thing that breaks. A good rule of thumb is to save 1.75% of your purchase price annually. Here is an example:

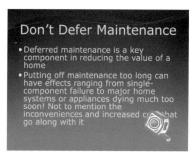

- Purchase price of home: $325,000

- Annual savings for maintenance = $325,000 x 0.0175 = $5,688

- Monthly savings for maintenance = $5,688 ÷ 12 = $474 per month

The key is having a maintenance budget saved. Your maintenance budget is critical to your enjoyment of your property and for maintaining and increasing the resale value of the property. Putting off maintenance can turn a small inexpensive problem into a large expensive one. Most people put off maintenance because they feel they just cannot afford it. Choosing to defer

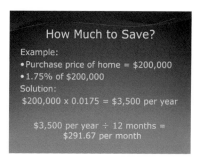

maintenance comes down to a financial decision: you either spend some money now or spend more money later; the choice is yours. Failing to repair a bad roof can cause major damage to a home over time. The average cost of major roof repair can range from $2,000 to $4,800. Most of us do not have this amount of money sitting around. That is why you need to save for repairs. If you do not have the money to fix your roof, paying for this necessary repair can put you into a financial tailspin. If you do not address the problem in a timely manner, much more damage could occur, creating an even larger financial impact. If you buy within your means and you factor in your maintenance budget, you will have the money to be able to do repairs when needed. A maintenance budget brings peace of mind.

When the time comes to sell your home, remember this slogan from the real estate industry, "The home will never sell until it is the best-priced property in the best condition in that given neighborhood." Make sure that will describe your home when it comes time to sell.

• Prioritize Your Maintenance

Keep a running maintenance list for your home. When you notice something that could use replacement or repair, put it on the list. Once you have several repairs on the list, give each item a priority ranking. What is the most important item to take care of first? Generally, you should first perform the repairs that are going to protect the structural integrity of your home. Next come repairs to maintain the appearance of your home and finally, additional improvements that you wish to make. Priorities may change when you revisit the list after a few months. If you track your maintenance needs and plan accordingly, you will be prepared for most repairs that will come up. What if several unexpected things go wrong at the same time? Prioritize them; decide what is most important and know that as soon as you have saved enough for repairs, you will call on that qualified, licensed, bonded, insured professional to fix those components. Your real estate agent may have suggestions for items to add to your maintenance list or how to prioritize needs based on his or her professional opinion and experience, so it is a good idea to get their input. But remember, the ultimate decision on what you fix and when is your responsibility.

Use Only Insured Service Providers

When hiring someone to perform repairs, many people will go with the cheapest person possible because they do not have money set aside for maintenance. By budgeting for maintenance, you also avoid the potential liability of hiring someone who may not be the most qualified for the job. You need to make sure that only insured service providers work on your property. Why? Home repairs are not without some risk. If you hire an unlicensed, uninsured contractor and she or he ends up getting hurt while in your home doing repairs, who is liable? You are, as the home-owner. That is right. You might end up having to pay for that person's care following an accident in your home. This is one reason why professional companies sometimes charge more than unlicensed fix-it workers—they need to cover the cost of insurance. You want to ensure that anybody who steps foot in your home to do any repairs is licensed and insured, and be sure to confirm their license and their worker's compensation insurance. You can look up some contractors' licenses online here: http://www.cslb.ca.gov/. Remember, if somebody is trimming your tree and falls and breaks his neck, you are liable. So please, please, please, do not just go with the cheapest person possible.

After Close of Escrow, What Role Does Your Agent Play?

You invested time and effort to find an experienced agent that you could trust. Reward their integrity and service by staying loyal to them. At the same time, they should earn your continued loyalty. Your agent should stick around with you for the long-term.

One way to keep in touch with your agent is to ask him or her to follow up on your escrow overage check. Remember that almost all escrows result in some amount refunded back to the buyer, because the estimated closing costs are often higher than the real costs. Most buyers should expect a refund between a few hundred dollars and a thousand dollars. Your agent might even decide to deliver the check to you in person to see how you are doing in the new home.

Healthy Homeowner Checkup

Talk to your agent and schedule a semi-annual or annual healthy homeowner checkup. Your real estate agent is trained to help you spot maintenance issues and improvements that will maintain

Healthy Homeowner Checkups

• Is your insurance coverage enough based on improvements to the home and the local economy?
• Check your list of maintenance issues
• Visit the city & county offices for updates on the community

and increase the value in your home. Use your agent's expertise to your advantage; there is no cost for this! Your agent wants to continue his or her relationship with you and welcomes the opportunity to come meet with you. If you live in an area with fire concerns, you might not notice how high the grass around your house is getting. At a healthy homeowner checkup, your real estate agent will look at your property with fresh eyes and tell you that cutting the high grass around your house right away is of the utmost importance. If your neighborhood is threatened with a situation like the San Diego fires, the Simi Valley fires, or the Oakland Hills fires, this one thing might make the difference in saving your home.

Once you purchase your home, you will probably make some changes to the house and property. Whether you modify the property right away or over a period of time, this may have an impact on your insurance coverage. Perhaps you have changed your kitchen countertops from tile to granite, upgraded the bathroom fixtures, and upgraded the appliances in the kitchen. Those are some very expensive upgrades, which have increased the value of your home and its contents. However, when you bought your property, you got insurance based on its value at that time. If you are not paying for enough replacement insurance, which is a minimal annual cost, you will not be able to rebuild your home the way it was if some tragedy strikes. Your real estate agent can also help you figure out a reasonable replacement value for which your home should be insured. This value is based on both the economy and your improvements. The checkup does not have to take all day. Take an hour with your agent and go through the house to make sure that your maintenance and insurance are up to date.

If you choose not to do an annual homeowner checkup, check in with your insurance agent annually in any case. One way to remember to do this is by using your impound account to remind you. When you get the statement from your impound account and you see that the amount for insurance has been dispersed, that means your insurance was just paid. Let that be a reminder for you to check in with your insurance agent.

Growing Communities and How They Affect Property Values

Another annual activity should be a trip down to city hall. There is always something going on within your city that most people do not know about. There may be a new development project with a required public disclosure, which may only be have been required to be given to those living within a 300-foot radius of the project. There may be plans for your neighborhood that will affect you. You may not hear about them until the project breaks ground and it is too late. Your city works for you. They represent you. So go down there and find out what they are doing that might affect your lifestyle and your quiet enjoyment of your home.

One key place to check is the local planning department. See what they are planning! Another place to check is the school district. Are there any new schools or changes to schools planned?

? ■ Ask the Expert

Question: If you buy a property with an FHA loan, can you rent it out?

Answer: If you have FHA financing for an owner-occupied property, the guidelines stipulate that you need to occupy the property within 60 days of funding for it to be considered a non-fraudulent transaction. If you can document a change of circumstances, then you can rent that property out. Be truthful about this, because if you do lie, you might be charged with intent to defraud a federally chartered institution.

Where are they? Find out what the test scores are for your local schools. Even if you do not have kids yourself, this will affect your resale value. If the schools in your community are going downhill, get involved. Good schools help maintain property values in a neighborhood.

• Compound Interest

Our current lending scenario has not been around for all that long. After the Great Depression, mortgages typically had a maximum of ten years of financing. What did that generation do? They paid off their loan, and then had a "deed-burning" party! Everybody would get together, have a cocktail, and they would watch the deed burn. Only then would they call themselves homeowners. We all like to consider ourselves homeowners once we close escrow; however, miss two payments and you will discover very quickly who is truly in charge.

Save Money with the Power of Compound Interest
- Compound interest is when you earn interest on your interest
- Over time this has a huge positive effect

Compound Interest Example
- Susan is 20 years old, and makes one $5,000 contribution to a Roth IRA
  - She and earns an average 8% annual return
  - She never withdraws any money
- She will have $160,000 by the time she retires at age 65
- If she does the same thing at age 39, she would only have $40,000 when she retires
- **Time is the key factor in the power of compounding**

We did not see much of our current paradigm of 30-year mortgages until after World War II and creation of the GI Bill. That is when home values really started to take off. If you want to aggressively build equity and value in your home and pay it off early, you have the flexibility to make a higher payment each month or make biweekly payments, and turn a 30-year mortgage into a 15- or 20-year loan. Only 3% of people are disciplined enough to do this. Paying off your mortgage sooner can save you thousands of dollars over the life of the loan. The bigger the loan, the greater the savings when you pay it off early.

Here is an example of how biweekly payments can save you money. Using a $250,000 loan amount with a 5% fixed interest rate:

- Paying monthly, you make 12 payments of $1,342.05 or a total of $16,104.60 for the year. The total interest you will pay over the life of the loan is $233,139.46

- If you pay half that amount every two weeks (biweekly), you make 26 payments of $671.03, or $17446.78 for the year. The total interest you will pay over the life of the loan is $188,722.13. That is a savings of $44,417.33 over the life of the loan!

- Note: Making payments biweekly is equivalent to making one extra payment in a year. This is because, instead of paying the full monthly amount 12 times in a year, you are paying half of that amount 26 times (not just 24 times) in a year. That results in the equivalent of one extra mortgage payment in a year and saves you $44,417.33.

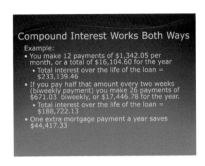

Compound Interest Works Both Ways
Example:
- You make 12 payments of $1,342.05 per month, or a total of $16,104.60 for the year
  - Total interest over the life of the loan = $233,139.46
- If you pay half that amount every two weeks (biweekly payment) you make 26 payments of $671.03 biweekly, or $17,446.78 for the year.
  - Total interest over the life of the loan = $188,722.13
- One extra mortgage payment a year saves $44,417.33

Now, because 97% of people do not pay more than the minimum mortgage payment, many lenders are not set up to accept biweekly payments. If you pay these lenders $671 instead of the expected $1,342.05, they are going to send the payment back to you and say it is short. How can you fix this? There are a couple of ways. One way is to be invited. Lenders that can do biweekly mortgages will invite you to convert your loan into this. There may be a $300-$400 set-up fee, and a small accounting fee that you pay on a monthly basis to do this.

Here is another way to accomplish the same thing. If your house payment is $1,200 a month, you can add one-twelfth that amount—$100—more to each payment. Let the lender know that the $100 is for additional principal only. If you write principal reduction only on the check, the lender cannot apply the extra amount to a shortage in the impound account or something else without you having remedy. What you are doing is effectively creating the equivalent of a biweekly mortgage. All a biweekly mortgage does is provide an extra payment every year. By taking this simple step, you will shave off approximately five years off the life of your loan and reduce the amount you pay toward interest over the loan's duration. Adding additional money to your payments will of course take off even more time.

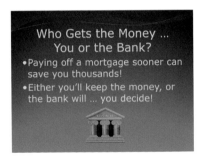

Who Gets the Money ... You or the Bank?
- Paying off a mortgage sooner can save you thousands!
- Either you'll keep the money, or the bank will ... you decide!

You can easily find mortgage or amortization calculators online and play with the numbers to see how different payments would affect your loan period and the amount of interest you will pay overall. By paying your mortgage off faster, you are effectively lowering your interest rate, because interest rates are calculated based on the entire life of the loan. For example, if you get a rate of 4.5% for a 30-year fixed-rate loan, you can actually get your effective interest rate down to 2% by paying extra on your mortgage. The interest is based on what you borrow and how fast the lender expects you to pay it back in full.

An Example of Compound Interest

Here is another example of how you can use compound interest to increase your financial health. What age will your child be at retirement? Let us say 65 years old for this example. Start an account for your five-year-old and put $50 a month into your child's account. How much will your child have at retirement age if we use an industry average rate of return of 8% over this 60-year period? $895,361.

Ask the Expert

Question: How can a first-time homebuyer know that the professionals they hire are working in their best interest?

Answer: Unfortunately, there is no decisive test, but there are ways to make sure that you do not choose a problematic agent. The first step is to go to www.dre.ca.gov and look up your potential agent's license with the Department of Real Estate to make sure that the license is valid and there are no disciplinary actions against them. It is also a good idea to ask to see proof that the broker carries current errors and omissions insurance. You also want to ask for references, and then make sure to call those references and ask them about their experience with the professional and how that person handled any problems with escrow. If you do all this, you will have eliminated a large number of unscrupulous agents. These steps will mitigate certain problems, but you cannot eliminate risk altogether. In the end, protect yourself by reading and understanding everything before you sign it.

What would be the result if the payment were increased to $100 a month using the same factors? Your child will have $1,790,711. Why not start a child with an interest earning account now by saving $100 a month? Relinquish it to them when they graduate college, get a job, and can continue to make payments. Whether your child becomes an educator, artist in Paris, or athlete, $100 a month is a small amount to pay toward retirement. Your child will be able to retire at only $100 a month because you started a retirement account at the ripe old age of five. Compounding interest is the eighth wonder of the world. Start early because the only way to make up time is with significantly more monthly savings, which for most, is not an option.

Go Green

There are many things you can do to help the environment and your community. In most cases, these changes will also save you money because of increased energy efficiency. One easy thing to do is to use fluorescent light bulbs. The new fluorescent bulbs look better, last longer and they will save you money because they use far less energy than incandescent bulbs to provide the

Go Green!
- Fluorescent bulbs
- Use energy efficient appliances
- Use dishwasher and clothes washer only when full
- Install low-flow shower heads
- Use a hot water re-circulation pump
- Recycle, reduce, reuse and compost

same amount of light. Another easy way to save energy is to only run dishwashers and clothes washers when they are full. Low-flow showerheads will save you money on heating and water bills. In a state where drought is a constant threat, saving water is always a good thing. You may also wish to purchase a hot water recirculation pump, which will give you instant hot water. This one is an investment but it does pay dividends in the long run.

Participate in local reduce, reuse and recycling programs and compost your garden and food waste whenever possible. Reducing the amount you consume and the amount of waste you create will save you money on garbage costs and benefit the environment.

Whether you are a homeowner or a tenant, local utility companies contract with professionals to come and inspect your home to see what you can do to make it more energy efficient. Every time

❓ Ask the Expert

Question: Is a real estate agent the same thing as a REALTOR®?

Answer: You do not have to be a REALTOR® to be a licensed real estate agent. The National Association of REALTORS®, the California Association of REALTORS® and local boards of REALTORS® are professional associations for real estate agents and brokers. To become a REALTOR®, a real estate agent must agree to a high standard of ethics and pay a membership fee. The California Department of Real Estate is the state agency that handles licensing and enforcement of real estate agents in California.

you pay your utility bill or your gas bill, a small portion is set aside for this program. If you meet certain income thresholds, you may receive incentives to retrofit your home to make it more energy efficient and save on your monthly utility bills.

• Hazardous Waste Materials

You must properly dispose of old computers and other technology, batteries, paint, hazardous waste and cleaners. The county spends millions of dollars cleaning up illegal dumping. Most local refuse companies have programs available to help homeowners responsibly dispose of hazardous waste. Contact your local refuse company or check online to find places in your area that collect different types of hazardous waste.

• Becoming a Real Estate Investor

Some of you might be interested in becoming real estate investors. It is important to understand that this is not a part-time occupation. Many of those that brought on the mortgage meltdown were inexperienced investors that purchased too many overvalued properties with little interest in the neighborhoods where those properties were located. There is a lot of competition out there among investors. It is not unusual to find investors that literally look at 150 homes a week. They look quickly because they know exactly what to look for, and they get to know the inventory intimately. From these 150 homes, they will narrow the possibilities down to a list of ten homes maximum that meet certain criteria. Then they will go in and invest, but they know down to the penny what they can afford to pay for the property. If the price goes a penny over this dollar figure, they do not pursue it because they are so disciplined. For investors, it is not a personal, emotional decision; it is just an investment. Therefore, investors look at properties in a completely different manner than do most homebuyers.

Getting support with investing can help a lot. You could join one of the many investors clubs that exist. There are also online classes available, many of them free. The best investors are looking at a long-term strategy, not trying to get rich quick. The get-rich-quick people are the ones that flip properties. In 2008–2009, investors were able to buy properties and flip them to make profits of $20,000 or more. Today these same investors are happy to get $10,000 to $15,000 per transaction because the competition is that fierce.

The Real Estate Investors Association website (www.nationalreia.com) has lots of information and is a great resource for individuals interested in real estate investment.

• Get Involved in Your Neighborhood

Why should you get involved in your neighborhood? You need to be informed about changes in your community because they can affect your home and its surroundings. It is important to pay attention to local news, as well as your elected officials—make sure that your government representatives are truly representing you and your community. And now that you are a homeowner, working to improve your community will also help you financially by maintaining or improving property values in your neighborhood.

Your Home, Your Community
•How Can You Get Involved? Volunteer!
 •Neighborhood Watch
 •Parks & Recreation
 •Senior centers
 •Local non-profits
 •Animal shelters
 •Schools

A website that can help you find volunteer opportunities in your neighborhood is www.servenet.org. You can also look for local volunteering organizations. Most communities have organizations that identify volunteer opportunities for residents. If you have older children, you can volunteer with them. Most high schools require 40 hours of community service to graduate. What better way to spend time with your teenager than volunteering in your community?

Neighborhood Watch

You will also have the opportunity to meet some of your neighbors when you become involved, which will build a stronger community and ensure that you have people nearby who are keeping an eye on your house when you are away. A neighborhood watch can play a big role in maintaining and increasing security in a neighborhood. Neighbors talk to each other, they get to know each other, and they look out for each other.

If you do not know your neighbors and keep in regular contact with them, when you notice a rented moving truck parked about four doors down from your house, you might think offhandedly, "Oh, that family must be moving." Because you have never met that neighbor, you ignore what is happening and mind your own business. When that family comes home to find that all their worldly goods have been stolen, they will wonder, "What happened? Didn't anybody see anything?" Had you known your neighbors, you may have been able to prevent this tragedy. Neighborhood Watch programs are a very, very powerful deterrent to crime. They might be considered essential for creating sustainable communities. You can get involved with Neighborhood Watch by going to www.nnwi.org. If your neighborhood does not currently have a Neighborhood Watch program, be the one to establish it! In addition to getting to know your neighbors better, think of the impact you can have on quality of life for the entire neighborhood.

Parks and Recreation

A parks and recreation program is another great way you can get involved with your community. When I was a community council member, I was fortunate to have the opportunity to start a parks and recreation program in my hometown. The program was called "Party Partners." We threw a party every week for local developmentally disabled citizens. For most of the participants, the Friday party was the highlight of their week. There was food, cake and ice cream, music and danc-ing. The children truly just beamed. Their parents would tell us how grateful they were that we started the program. Participation in Party Pardners often allowed a child to become excited and engaged for the first time. There is nothing better than giving back where you are genuinely involved with your community and its people, when you feel that the hour you gave truly made a difference. You may never know the impact that you had on somebody else.

Other Opportunities to Get Involved

Most local animal shelters need volunteers to help at the shelter and care for the animals. If you love animals, this is a great opportunity. Schools also need help and you can volunteer at them. You could start a neighborhood newsletter. While setting up a neighborhood watch, an agent created a newsletter that highlighted the gifts and talents of the people in the neighborhood. It went out on a monthly basis and everybody had a spot promoting his or her services. Everyone paid just a little bit of money to make the newsletter happen, to the benefit of the entire community.

• You Are Not Your Neighbor

Always remember to avoid comparing yourself to your neighbor. We are all familiar with this behavior. It is difficult as a homeowner to keep a budget and save 1.75% toward repairs, pay down your debt faster, and save for your child's education and retirement, when you see the neighbor across the street pull up in a new car. This happened more often when the market was going up and people could use their homes as ATMs. Looking at the neighbor, it may seem that she or he is more successful than you are. It is difficult to see the new car and know that your neighbors are going to the river every other weekend. You see a sand rail (dune buggy) and a new toy hauler parked out front of their home, while you are living modestly. But many of the people who were spending frivolously have now lost their homes.

We need to take a step back from how things were in the first decade of the 2000s, recognize the paradigm shift, and evaluate what is most important. Do you want to have the new car and new toys? Or is more important to protect your investment, to have a roof over our head, peace in your heart, and the ability to take care of your parents and your children? You have different priorities, because you are the new sustainable homeowner, creating stability for your community.

Summary

At the conclusion of this course, the reader should be able to demonstrate mastery of the course objectives and learning outcomes listed here.

• Course Objectives

At the conclusion of this course, readers should be able to reflect upon their learning and have confidence in their ability to accomplish the following:

1. Complete a budget worksheet, including calculating monthly living expenses.
2. List three important questions to ask when interviewing real estate agents and lenders in order to identify professionals with strong ethics.
3. Calculate monthly gross and net income, and state what they could safely afford for a monthly payment.
4. State approximate amounts needed for a down payment and closing costs for purchase of a home.
5. Calculate the amount of money to be set aside in savings every month for maintenance after purchasing a home.

• Learning Outcomes

After completing this course, the reader should be able to:

Module 1: Budgeting
- Describe why budgeting is important in achieving financial goals
- Itemize expenses in a budget.
- Explain the differences between a good budget and a bad budget
- Complete the budget worksheet

Module 2: Borrowing
- Describe how to find a good real estate agent and loan originator
- List three important questions to ask when interviewing real estate agents and lenders to identify professionals with strong ethics

- Calculate their front-end and back-end ratios for a sample home purchase
- Identify where to get more information/help with buyers' assistance programs.

Module 3: Buying

- Explain the meaning of a contract/offer to purchase as a legal document
- List common buyer expenses incurred in escrow
- State approximate amounts needed for a down payment and closing costs for purchase of a nearby home.
- Describe an escrow calendar and how it works

Module 4: Beyond

- Calculate the amount s/he should be saving every month for maintenance.
- Report what an agent should continue to do after home purchase.
- List two ways to get involved with the community.

Evaluation

College: _____

Date: _____, 20_____

Instructor: _____

Please circle your response:

1. The instructor was knowledgeable and up-to-date on the course subject.   Yes   No   N/A

2. The instructor was well organized and easy to understand.   Yes   No   N/A

3. The instructor digressed from the course subject with an excessive amount of war stories, jokes, personal experiences, etc.   Yes   No   N/A

4. The instructor promoted the sale of products (i.e., tapes, text, etc.) during the educational instruction portion of the course.   Yes   No   N/A

5. The educational material (outline, text, video, etc.) was well prepared and easy to understand.   Yes   No   N/A

6. The handout materials, if any, were or will be useful to me.   Yes   No   N/A

7. The presentation increased my knowledge of the course subject.   Yes   No   N/A

8. I will be able to use the knowledge learned in this course to better serve and protect consumers.   Yes   No   N/A

9. I would enroll in another presentation or course such as this in the future.   Yes   No   N/A

10. Taking all items into consideration, I would rate this course as (circle one):

    Excellent   Above Average   Good   Fair   Poor

11. Do you have any suggestions to improve future courses?   Yes   No   N/A
    If YES, please list below.

12. Would you like to be contacted by a Real Estate Education Center representative? If YES, please provide your name and number.   Yes   No   N/A

    Name: _____

    Daytime Phone Number: _____

13. Comments/Suggestions:

If you prefer, you may send your evaluation to the

Real Estate Education Center
San Francisco City College—Downtown Campus
88 Fourth Street, Room 324
San Francisco, CA 94103

Or email to: Information@CaliforniaFinancialLiteracy.org

Self-Assessment Rubric

Presenter Name: _____

Date of Activity: _____

Participant Name: _____

This rubric is used by the Instructor to access the individual or collective success of the workshop for the participants.

CATEGORY	PROGRESS ACHIEVED			
	Little Progress Achieved	Some Progress Achieved	Substantial Progress Achieved	Great Progress Achieved
Ethics of Real Estate Professionals	Participant is unable to identify any behaviors associated with or expected from a real estate professional	Participant is able to identify at least one attribute or question that will provide an ethics assessment tool for behaviors associated with real estate professionals	Participant is able to identify at least two attributes or questions that will provide ethics assessment tools for behaviors associated with real estate professionals	Participant is able to identify three or more attributes or questions that will provide an ethics assessment tool for behaviors associated with real estate professionals
Licensing Confirmation	Participant is unable to name any governmental licensing units for ascertaining the license status of a real estate professional	Participant is able to name the California Department of Real Estate as a source of information pertaining to the license status of a real estate professional	Participant is able to name and identify the California Department of Real Estate website (http://dre.ca.gov) as a source for information pertaining to a real estate professional's license status, and disciplinary actions, if any	Participant is able to name and identify two or more of the following licensing or regulating departments regarding real estate activities: 1) Department of Real Estate; 2) Department of Financial Institutions; 3) Department of Insurance (Escrow); 4) U.S. HUD; 5) Instructor's Discretion
Budgeting - Income	Participant unable to identify the source(s), amount(s) and total monthly income for the household	Participant is able to identify at least one source and amount of monthly income for the household	Participant is able to identify all earned sources, amount(s) and total of monthly income for the household	Participant is able to identify all sources, amount(s) and total of monthly income for the household including: wages, independent contracts, dividends, rental income, dependent income, alimony, child support, and other government programs.

Self-Assessment Rubric, *continued*

CATEGORY	PROGRESS ACHIEVED			
	Little Progress Achieved	Some Progress Achieved	Substantial Progress Achieved	Great Progress Achieved
Budgeting - Expense	Participant is unable to identify, list or associate broad categories of monthly expenses	Participant is able to identify and list amounts of monthly housing expenses including: rent, loan payment, insurance, property taxes, home owner association fees	Participant is able to identify and list all monthly housing expenses plus all other living expenses in detail	Participant is able to compare monthly expenses to monthly income and reflect on that computation. Participant exhibits critical thinking behaviors.
Borrowing	Participant is unable to differentiate between gross and net monthly wages.	Participant is able to differentiate between gross and net monthly wages	Participant is able to calculate percentage/ratio of rental housing expenses to net monthly income	Participant is able to calculate percentage/ratio of home ownership expenses (Principle, Interest, Taxes, & Insurance) to gross monthly income
Buying	Participant does not see a window or pathway for home ownership	Participant is able to list and use three buying-related vocabulary words	Participant is able to identify at least three potential sources of financing for home ownership: 1) HUD; 2) conventional banking; 3) Mortgage brokers/bankers; 4) VA/CAL-VET; 5) Other	Participant is able to reflect upon and articulate the benefits of home ownership in comparison to renting vies a vies his/her personal lifestyle choices.
Beyond	Participant does not see the necessity or benefit of post-purchase reflection and planning	Participant is able to list at least three major home maintenance projects that can be anticipated in a 7- to 30-year home ownership span.	Participant is able to identify at least three community service or support organizations in their area	Participant is able to articulate and reflect on the value of stable home ownership and its relationship to stable communities
Evaluation	Participant walks out of the workshop within two hours of start	Participant does NOT complete Course Evaluation request	Participant does complete the Course Evaluation request	Participant receives a "Certificate of Completion" upon conclusion of the workshop

Multiple-Choice Quiz

Donna Grogan, Real Estate Program Chair at El Camino College in Torrance, California, created the following multiple-choice quiz.

1. Which of the following is NOT one of the main subjects of this financial literacy course?

    a. Balancing
    b. Borrowing
    c. Budgeting
    d. Buying

2. Money problems and lack of financial planning

    a. Cause stress about retirement
    b. Often lead to divorce
    c. Usually result in lack of funding for students to attend college
    d. All of the above

3. Good financial planning includes tracking all of the following *except*:

    a. Debt ratio
    b. Front-end and back-end ratios
    c. FICO score
    d. Property tax assessor identification number

4. The total monthly payment calculation used for loan qualification includes

    a. Principal and interest (P & I)
    b. Taxes and insurance (T & I)
    c. Homeowners association (HOA) fees and private mortgage insurance (PMI) or a mortgage insurance premium (MIP)
    d. All of the above

5. How much should a buyer save each month in a reserve for ongoing maintenance (percentage times the price of the property divided by 12 months in a year)?

    a. 0.5 % $100 per month minimum
    b. 1.75 % $300–$500 per month for an average property
    c. 2.5 % $800–$1,000 per month for an average property
    d. 5% $1,200–$1,500 per month maximum for any property

6. Which of the following loans allows a buyer to place only 3.5% of the purchase price as a cash down payment?

    a. CalHFA
    b. FHA
    c. Reverse mortgage
    d. VA

7. The front-end ratio is calculated by which of the following methods?

    a. Total income minus total liabilities divided by net income
    b. Net income less net expenses times 30%
    c. Total housing expense divided by gross income
    d. Total expenses (housing and debt/loans) divided by net income

8. A goal for financial maturity is to have a FICO score of:

    a. 250–400
    b. 400–600
    c. 640 or higher
    d. 800 or higher

9. All of the following questions should be asked by a borrower about any and all proposed charges or fees, EXCEPT:

    a. Who is charging the fee?
    b. What can I ask the licensed agents to pay from their commission and fees?
    c. Why are they charging this?
    d. When does it apply?

10. A CalVet loan program obtains the funds it loans to a borrower from which source?

    a. Veterans Affairs military funds
    b. The Veterans Administration federal grants program
    c. Bonds sold to investors to allow veterans to buy homes
    d. The California state budget allocation from property taxes used only for U.S. veterans

11. The borrower should have:

    a. Two months worth of reserves for impounds and expenses
    b. No more than 3-5 credit cards
    c. Credit card loan balances of 30% or less of the credit limit
    d. All of the above

12. Your FICO score does not include which of the following?

    a. Credit card debt

    b. Utility bills

    c. Car loans

    d. Student loans

13. A buyer should expect to be familiar with all of the following *except*

    a. California Association of REALTORS® (CAR®) forms

    b. Disclosure forms

    c. Government loan program forms (FNMA 1003—loan application, etc.)

    d. Loan forms for speakers of English as a second language

14. What should a homebuyer include in his or her budget?

    a. Future income tax refunds expected to be received from owning a property

    b. Average rent payment over the past 10 years

    c. Housing expenses, projected income and consumer debt

    d. Amount of equity in autos, boats and motor homes if applicable

15. Buyers can avoid problems with a potential property purchase if they take the time to do the following in advance:

    a. Interview the property's neighbors to get a feel for the community and to identify existing issues in the neighborhood

    b. Take a trip to city hall and local county offices to inquire about code violations on the property, permits and future development plans for the neighborhood and area

    c. Educate themselves about potential tax return refund amounts for the next ten years that can be used to make the house payment to pay the taxes and to pay the insurance

    d. Learn about the seller's existing loan to see what loan program was already on the property, and ask the seller if they are happy with their lender

16. After escrow has closed on a home purchase, financial sense is:

    a. Regular checkups for healthy homeownership

    b. No longer part of the process since once you own the home and are on the hook for the payments and expenses of the property

    c. Padding the escrow account so there is a reserve

    d. Disclosing the proceeds that would be received if a short sale were used in the future

17. A borrower is able to obtain greater financing by completing an 8-hour approved course for which type of loan?

    a. National veterans program

    b. Housing and Urban Development (HUD) loan program

    c. California FHA loan program

    d. National Cal-Vet loan program

18. It is wise to schedule a semi-annual or an annual healthy homeowner checkup to:

    a. Determine if there is enough insurance coverage on the property in light of improvements you have made

    b. Help you spot and prioritize maintenance needs

    c. Get advice from your real estate agent on improvements that you should make to increase your home's value

    d. All of the above

19. Regardless of the original repayment period of your loan, the goal is to:

    a. Not trigger an increase in the interest rate on the loan

    b. Lower the impound account reserves for the property

    c. Pay off the loan as quickly as possible

    d. Make minimum monthly payments for the entire term of the loan

20. Which of the following actions can a homeowner take to "go green"?

    a. Install a hot water re-circulating pump

    b. Recycle, reuse and compost

    c. Install low-flow shower heads and wash only full loads of dishes and clothes

    d. All of the above

Answers on page 75

Sample Participation Certificate

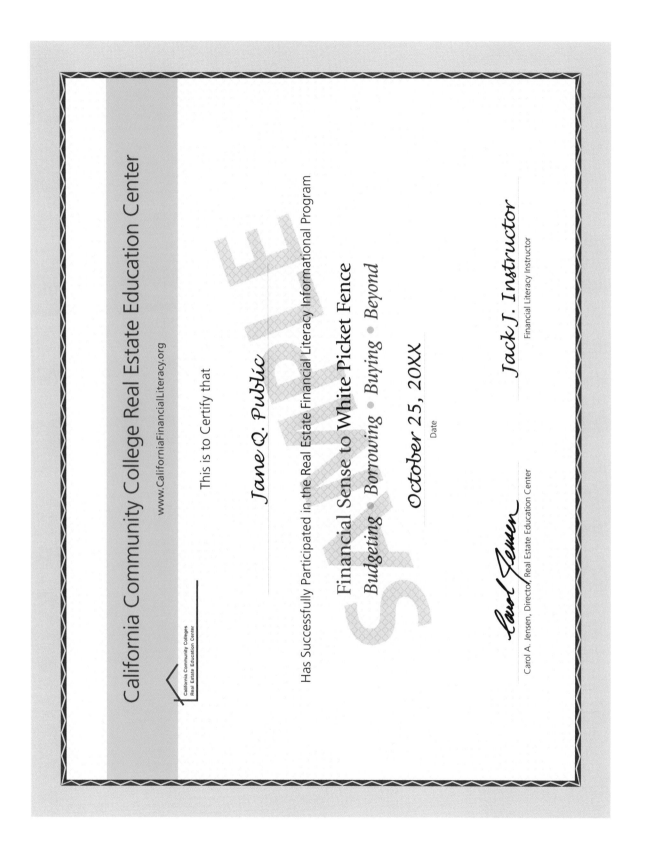

California Community College Real Estate Education Center

www.CaliforniaFinancialLiteracy.org

California Community Colleges
Real Estate Education Center

This is to Certify that

Jane Q. Public

Has Successfully Participated in the Real Estate Financial Literacy Informational Program

Financial Sense to White Picket Fence
Budgeting • Borrowing • Buying • Beyond

October 25, 20XX

Date

Jack J. Instructor

Financial Literacy Instructor

Carol Jensen

Carol A. Jensen, Director, Real Estate Education Center

• Multiple-Choice Quiz Answers

1. a. Balancing

2. d. All of the above

3. d. Property tax assessor identification number

4. d. All of the above

5. b. 1.75% $300-$500 per month for an average property

6. b. FHA

7. c. Total housing expense divided by gross income

8. c. 640 or higher

9. b. What can I ask the licensed agents to pay from their commission and fees?

10. c. Bonds sold to investors to allow veterans to buy homes

11. d. All of the above

12. b. Utility bills

13. d. Loan forms for speakers of English as a second language

14. b. Average rent payment over the past 10 years

15. c. Educate themselves about potential tax return refund amounts for the next ten years that can be used to make the house payment to pay the taxes

16. a. Regular checkups for healthy home ownership

17. b. Housing and Urban Development (HUD) loan program

18. d. All of the above

19. c. Pay off the loan as quickly as possible

20. d. All of the above

Websites / Resources

The California Department of Real Estate http://dre.ca.gov

The California Department of Real Estate 2011 Real Estate Law Book http://www.dre.ca.gov/pub_relaw.html

The California Business and Professions Code http://www.leginfo.ca.gov/.html/bpc_table_of_contents.html

The United States Department of Housing and Urban Development (HUD) http://hud.gov

The United States Department of Housing and Urban Development HUD 41552-2, "Lenders Guide to the Single Family Mortgage Insurance Process"

http://www.hud.gov/offices/adm/hudclips/handbooks/hsgh/4155.2/41552HSGH.pdf

The California Office of Real Estate Appraisers http://orea.ca.gov

California Association of REALTORS® http://car.org

National Association of Real Estate Brokers http://nareb.com

National Association of Hispanic Real Estate Professionals http://nahrep.org

Homeownership Education Learning Program (H.E.L.P.)™ http://freehomeownershiphelp.org

Making Home Affordable—The United States Department of the Treasury http://makinghomeaffordable.gov

Financial Stability—The Department of the Treasury http://financialstability.gov

Fannie Mae http://fanniemae.com

Freddie Mac http://freddiemac.com

Ginnie Mae—Your Path to Home Ownership http://www.ginniemae.gov/1_learn/h_i_c.asp?Section=YPTH

Hope Loan Portal http://hopeloanportal.org

The Federal Reserve Board http://federalreserve.com

California Financial Literacy http://CaliforniaFinancialLiteracy.org

California Community College Real Estate Education Center http://ccsf.edu/Real_estate_education_center

Bank Rate http://bankrate.com

Mortgage 101 http://mortgage101.com

Operation Hope http://operationhope.org

Internal Revenue Service http://irs.gov

The California Department of Financial Institutions http://www.dfi.ca.gov/caflm

The California Department of Insurance—Title Insurance and Escrow http://www.insurance

Annual Credit Report https://www.annualcreditreport.com

California Department of Corporations—Debt, Mortgage and Loan Calculators http://www.corp
.ca.gov/Education_Outreach/literacy/calculators

The National Association of Real Estate Brokers—Investment Division, Inc., Housing Counseling
Agency (NID-HCA) http://www.makingyourhomeaffordable.org and http://www.nidonline.org

National Council for Credit Counseling http://www.nfcc.org/

EconEdLink Compound Interest Calculator http://www.econedlink.org/interactives/EconEdLink
-interactive-tool-player.php?iid=2&full

Exhibits

Student Learning Outcomes for Module 1

Budgeting

At the completion of this module, students will be able to:

✔ Describe why budgeting is important in achieving financial goals

✔ Be able to list the things to track in a budget.

✔ Explain the differences between a good budget and a bad budget

✔ Know how to complete the budget worksheet

Budget Example A

Budgeting

Monthly Budget

INCOME—after tax	
Adult 1	$2283.00
Adult 2	$548.00
TOTAL INCOME	**$2831.00**

Expenses

Donations	$300.00
Groceries	$250.00–300.00
Rent	$855.00
Sewer, water, and trash	$30.50
Phone	$50.00
Electric and gas (on the high side)	$200.00
Gas for car	$120.00
Credit cards	$250.00
Internet	$30.00
Uncovered Medical Expenses	$75.00
Home supplies: paper goods, soap etc.	$125.00
Clothes (mostly from yard sales and thrift stores)	$30.00
Stamps	$8.00
Car insurance	$50.00
Car repairs and tags	$75.00
Haircuts	$20.00
Presents-birthdays, etc.	$50.00
Social and entertainment (incl eating out)	$100.00
Vacations	$0.00
TOTAL EXPENSES	**$2668.50**

Savings each month: **$162.50**

Budget Example B

Budgeting

Monthly Budget

INCOME	
Adult 1	$2300.00
Adult 2	$500.00
TOTAL INCOME	**$2800.00**

Expenses

Rent	$855
Food	$400
Utilities	$150
Car	$150
Entertainment	$50
Other	$50
TOTAL EXPENSES	**$1655**

෨ ෨ ෨ ෨

Analysis

1. What is good about Budget A? Budget B?

2. What is bad about Budget A? Budget B?

3. Do you think Budget A is a good reflection of what that family's actual spending will be?

4. Do you think Budget B is a good reflection of what that family's actual spending will be?

5. What are some categories that you would include in your budget that you don't see here?

Track Your Daily Spending for One Month or More

Example

Item	Cost	Method of Payment	Monthly Cost	Annual Cost
Coffee	$2.50	Debit Card	$50.00	$600
Soda	$1.00	Cash	$	$
Snacks	$3.50	Cash	$	$
Magazines/Books	$4.00	Debit	$	$
Cosmetics	$7.50	Credit Card	$	$

(Purchase coffee every day for 20 work days per month. It all adds up!)

Month of _____

Item	Cost	Method of Payment	Monthly Cost	Annual Cost
	$		$	$
	$		$	$
	$		$	$
	$		$	$
	$		$	$
	$		$	$
	$		$	$
	$		$	$
	$		$	$
	$		$	$
	$		$	$
	$		$	$
	$		$	$
	$		$	$
	$		$	$
	$		$	$
Keep tracking!	$		$	$

California Financial Literacy Month (CAFLM)
Web: www.dfi.ca.gov/caflm
Twitter: @CAFLM
Blog: http://caflm.blogs.ca.gov

Tips:
Use receipts to help you track all spending.
Track your transactions daily or as often as possible.
Make tracking a routine; log spending during lunch or every evening after dinner, etc.
Do what works for you. Track by hand on a printed sheet or track on an electronic spreadsheet.

Monthly Income and Expenses

GROSS INCOME PER MONTH _____

    Salary   _____

    Interest   _____

    Dividends   _____

    Other (_____)   _____

    Other (_____)   _____

LESS:

1. Tithe   _____

2. Tax (Est. - Incl. Fed., State, FICA) _____

    NET SPENDABLE INCOME _____

3. Housing   _____

    Mortgage (rent)   _____

    Insurance   _____

    Taxes   _____

    Electricity   _____

    Gas   _____

    Water   _____

    Sanitation   _____

    Telephone   _____

    Maintenance   _____

    Other (_____)   _____

    Other (_____)   _____

4. Food   _____

5. Automobile(s)   _____

    Payments   _____

    Gas and Oil   _____

    Insurance   _____

    License/Taxes   _____

    Maint./Repair/Replace _____

6. Insurance   _____

    Life   _____

    Medical   _____

    Other (_____)   _____

7. Debts   _____

    Credit Card   _____

    Loans and Notes   _____

    Other (_____)   _____

    Other (_____)   _____

8. Enter./Recreation   _____

    Eating Out   _____

    Baby Sitters   _____

    Activities/Trips   _____

    Vacation   _____

    Other (_____)   _____

    Other (_____)   _____

9. Clothing   _____

10. Savings   _____

11. Medical Expenses   _____

    Doctor   _____

    Dentist   _____

    Drugs   _____

    Other (_____)   _____

12. Miscellaneous   _____

    Toiletry, cosmetics   _____

    Beauty, barber   _____

    Laundry, cleaning   _____

    Allowances, lunches   _____

    Subscriptions   _____

    Gifts (incl. Christmas) _____

    Cash   _____

    Internet   _____

    Other (_____)   _____

    Other (_____)   _____

13. Investments   _____

14. School/Child Care   _____

    Tuition   _____

    Materials   _____

    Transportation   _____

    Day Care   _____

    Other (_____)   _____

TOTAL EXPENSES   _____

INCOME VERSUS EXPENSES

    Net Spendable Income   _____

    Less Expenses   _____

    _____

Budget Analysis

Per Year $_____

Per Month $_____

Net Spendable Income
Per Month $_____

MONTHLY PAYMENT CATEGORY	EXISTING BUDGET	MONTHLY GUIDELINE BUDGET	DIFFERENCE + OR -	NEW MONTHLY BUDGET
1. Tithe				
2. Tax				
Net Spendable Income (per month)	$_____	$_____	$_____	$_____
3. Housing				
4. Food				
5. Auto				
6. Insurance				
7. Debts				
8. Enter./Recreation				
9. Clothing				
10. Savings				
11. Medical				
12. Miscellaneous				
13. Investments				
14. School/Child Care				
Totals (Items 3-14)	$_____	$_____	/////////	$_____

Monthly Family Budget

	Total Projected Cost	Total Actual Cost	Total Difference
	$1,203	$1,317	($114)

Housing	Projected Cost	Actual Cost	Difference
Mortgage or rent	$1,000	$1,000 ⇨	$0
Second mortgage or	$0	$0 ⇨	$0
Phone	$62	$100 ⇨	-$38
Electricity	$44	$125 ⬇	-$81
Gas	$22	$35 ⇨	-$13
Water and sewer	$8	$8 ⇨	$0
Cable	$34	$39 ⇨	-$5
Waste removal	$10	$10 ⇨	$0
Maintenance or repairs	$23	$0 ⇨	$23
Supplies	$0	$0 ⇨	$0
Other	$0	$0 ⇨	$0
Total	$1,203	$1,317	($114)

Projected Monthly Income	
Income 1	$4,000
Income 2	$1,200
Extra income	$300
Total monthly income	$5,500

Actual Monthly Income	
Income 1	$4,000
Income 2	$1,200
Extra income	$300
Total monthly income	$5,500

Projected balance	$4,297
Actual balance	$4,183
Difference ⬇	($114)

Transportation	Projected Cost	Actual Cost	Difference
Vehicle 1 payment		⇨	$0
Vehicle 2 payment		⇨	$0
Bus/taxi fare		⇨	$0
Insurance		⇨	$0
Licensing		⇨	$0
Fuel		⇨	$0
Maintenance		⇨	$0
Other		⇨	$0
Total	$0	$0	$0

Insurance	Projected Cost	Actual Cost	Difference
Home		⇨	$0
Health		⇨	$0
Life		⇨	$0
Other		⇨	$0
Total	$0	$0	$0

Food	Projected Cost	Actual Cost	Difference
Groceries		⇨	$0
Dining out		⇨	$0
Other		⇨	$0
Total	$0	$0	$0

Children	Projected Cost	Actual Cost	Difference
Medical		⇨	$0
Clothing		⇨	$0
School tuition		⇨	$0
School supplies		⇨	$0
Organization dues or		⇨	$0
Lunch money		⇨	$0
Child care		⇨	$0
Toys/games		⇨	$0
Other		⇨	$0
Total	$0	$0	$0

Legal	Projected Cost	Actual Cost	Difference
Attorney		⇨	$0
Alimony		⇨	$0
Payments		⇨	$0
Other		⇨	$0
Total	$0	$0	$0

Savings/Investment	Projected Cost	Actual Cost	Difference
Retirement account		⇨	$0
Investment account		⇨	$0
College		⇨	$0
Other		⇨	$0
Total	$0	$0	$0

Loans	Projected Cost	Actual Cost	Difference
Personal		⇨	$0
Student		⇨	$0
Credit card		⇨	$0
Credit card		⇨	$0
Credit card		⇨	$0
Other		⇨	$0
Total	$0	$0	$0

Entertainment	Projected Cost	Actual Cost	Difference
Video/DVD		⇨	$0
CDs		⇨	$0
Movies		⇨	$0
Concerts		⇨	$0
Sporting events		⇨	$0
Live theater		⇨	$0
Other		⇨	$0
Total	$0	$0	$0

Taxes	Projected Cost	Actual Cost	Difference
Federal		⇨	$0
State		⇨	$0
Local		⇨	$0
Other		⇨	$0
Total	$0	$0	$0

Personal Care	Projected Cost	Actual Cost	Difference
Medical		⇨	$0
Hair/nails		⇨	$0
Clothing		⇨	$0
Dry cleaning		⇨	$0
Health club		⇨	$0
Organization dues/fees		⇨	$0
Other		⇨	$0
Total	$0	$0	$0

Pets	Projected Cost	Actual Cost	Difference
Food		⇨	$0
Medical		⇨	$0
Grooming		⇨	$0
Toys		⇨	$0
Other		⇨	$0
Total	$0	$0	$0

Gifts and Donations	Projected Cost	Actual Cost	Difference
Charity 1		⇨	$0
Charity 2		⇨	$0
Charity 3		⇨	$0
Total	$0	$0	$0

Know Your Monthly Income

Item	Monthly Income	Annual Income
Wages	$	$
Wages	$	$
Overtime	$	$
Bonuses	$	$
Commissions	$	$
Tips	$	$
Child Support	$	$
Social Security	$	$
Retirement/Pension	$	$
Gifts	$	$
Tax Refunds	$	$
Other income	$	$
Other income	$	$
Other income	$	$
Other income	$	$
TOTAL	$	$

Tips:
Deposit checks right away.
Balance your checking account regularly.
Organize your bills and tax information.
Assign priorities to your bills so you can reduce or eliminate some.

California Financial Literacy Month (CAFLM)
Web: www.dfi.ca.gov/caflm
Twitter: @CAFLM
Blog: http://caflm.blogs.ca.gov

Record Your Monthly Expenses

Item	Monthly Expenses (Average)	Fixed or Flexible Amount	Annual Expense
Mortgage/Rent	$	Fixed	$
Daycare/School	$	Fixed	$
Utilities (gas, electricity, etc.)	$		$
Telephone/s	$		$
Internet	$		$
Cable TV	$		$
Car Payment	$		$
Gasoline	$		$
Insurance	$		$
Parking	$		$
Medical	$		$
Gym	$		$
Groceries/Toiletries	$		$
Credit Card/s	$		$
Pet expenses	$		$
Loans (not mortgage or car)	$		$
Toiletries	$		$
Clothing/Uniforms	$		$
Dry Cleaning	$		$
Charitable	$		$
Gifts (average)	$		$
Savings/Retirement Accounts	$		$
Memberships	$		$
Other	$		$
Other	$		$
Other	$		$

California Financial Literacy Month (CAFLM)
Web: www.dfi.ca.gov/caflm
Twitter: @CAFLM
Blog: http://caflm.blogs.ca.gov

Exhibit 9: Record Your Monthly Expenses (Supplement for Module 1: Budgeting): 1 of 1

Student Learning Outcomes for Module 2

Borrowing

At the completion of this module, students will be able to:

✔ Describe how to find a good real estate agent and loan originator

✔ List three important questions to ask when interviewing real estate agents and lenders to identify professionals with strong ethics

✔ Calculate their front-end and back-end ratios for a sample home purchase

✔ Identify where to get more information or help with buyers' assistance programs.

Calculating Front-End and Back-End Ratios for Qualifying for a Loan

Borrowing

Your front-end and back-end ratios are one of the fist things a potential lender will look at in deciding if you qualify for a loan. You should know how to find yours.

Front-End Ratios

The Front-end ratio shows the lender what percentage or your total income your mortgage payment (PITI) will be: Most conventional lenders do not want to see a front-end ratio of more than 28% to 35% depending on the down payment, savings and other important compensating factors. FHA loans range from 30% to 35% as well using the same compensation factors for the higher ratio. Borrowers are always encouraged to know their budget in order to determine ratios that are right for them.

Calculate your Front-End Ratio:

- The monthly combined gross income in my household is $_____

- A monthly mortgage payment that I think I could afford is $_____

  Monthly Mortgage ÷ Gross Income = _____ or _____ %

  This is your Front-End Ratio

Back-End Ratio

The back-end ratio shows the lender how much of your income is tied up in paying back all debt. It is also expressed as a percentage. Back-end ratios are higher than front-end ratios. For most conventional loans, the back-end ratio is 45%. For an FHA loan, the back-end ratio is 43%.

Calculate your Back-End Ratio:

- The monthly combined gross income in my household is $_____

- Total of all monthly loan payments (including mortgage) $_____

  Monthly Loan Payments ÷ Gross Income = _____ or _____ %

  This is your Back-End Ratio

Interview Questions
for Real Estate Professionals

Borrowing

One of the most important decisions you can make in the lending and home buying process is who you choose to represent you. You should talk to AT LEAST TWO different real estate agents and AT LEAST TWO different lenders/loan originators before deciding with whom you want to work.

Here are some good questions to ask, but feel free to add your own.

What to ask a loan originator

1. May I see a copy of your real estate license and proof of Mortgage Loan Originator License Endorsement Certificate?

2. May I see a copy of your Error & Omissions Insurance Policy? (Optional, as he/she may be self insured)

3. May I see your resume and/or get referrals from past clients?

4. With which first time home buyer programs are you familiar with? Which ones have you helped clients use and with which have you completed transactions?

5. Are there any financial, marketing, or commission arrangements between you and the professionals to whom you are referring me?

What to ask a real estate agent

1. May I see a copy of your real estate license?

2. May I see a copy of your error & omissions Insurance Policy?

3. May I see your resume and/or receive referrals from past clients?

4. With which first time home buyer programs are you familiar? Which transactions have you helped clients use and complete?

5. What sets you apart from your competition?

6. Do you or your company receive any additional monies or referral fees for directing me to a lender, title, or escrow company? This must be disclosed in writing.

OMB Approval No. 2502-0265

A. **Settlement Statement (HUD-1)**

B. Type of Loan				
1. ☐ FHA 2. ☐ RHS 3. ☐ Conv. Unins. 4. ☐ VA 5. ☐ Conv. Ins.	6. File Number:	7. Loan Number:	8. Mortgage Insurance Case Number:	

C. Note: This form is furnished to give you a statement of actual settlement costs. Amounts paid to and by the settlement agent are shown. Items marked "(p.o.c.)" were paid outside the closing; they are shown here for informational purposes and are not included in the totals.

D. Name & Address of Borrower:	E. Name & Address of Seller:	F. Name & Address of Lender:

G. Property Location:	H. Settlement Agent:	I. Settlement Date:
	Place of Settlement:	

J. Summary of Borrower's Transaction		K. Summary of Seller's Transaction	
100. Gross Amount Due from Borrower		**400. Gross Amount Due to Seller**	
101. Contract sales price		401. Contract sales price	
102. Personal property		402. Personal property	
103. Settlement charges to borrower (line 1400)		403.	
104.		404.	
105.		405.	
Adjustment for items paid by seller in advance		**Adjustments for items paid by seller in advance**	
106. City/town taxes to		406. City/town taxes to	
107. County taxes to		407. County taxes to	
108. Assessments to		408. Assessments to	
109.		409.	
110.		410.	
111.		411.	
112.		412.	
120. Gross Amount Due from Borrower		**420. Gross Amount Due to Seller**	
200. Amounts Paid by or in Behalf of Borrower		**500. Reductions In Amount Due to Seller**	
201. Deposit or earnest money		501. Excess deposit (see instructions)	
202. Principal amount of new loan(s)		502. Settlement charges to seller (line 1400)	
203. Existing loan(s) taken subject to		503. Existing loan(s) taken subject to	
204.		504. Payoff of first mortgage loan	
205.		505. Payoff of second mortgage loan	
206.		506.	
207.		507.	
208.		508.	
209.		509.	
Adjustments for items unpaid by seller		**Adjustments for items unpaid by seller**	
210. City/town taxes to		510. City/town taxes to	
211. County taxes to		511. County taxes to	
212. Assessments to		512. Assessments to	
213.		513.	
214.		514.	
215.		515.	
216.		516.	
217.		517.	
218.		518.	
219.		519.	
220. Total Paid by/for Borrower		**520. Total Reduction Amount Due Seller**	
300. Cash at Settlement from/to Borrower		**600. Cash at Settlement to/from Seller**	
301. Gross amount due from borrower (line 120)		601. Gross amount due to seller (line 420)	
302. Less amounts paid by/for borrower (line 220)	( )	602. Less reductions in amount due seller (line 520)	( )
303. Cash ☐ From ☐ To Borrower		**603. Cash** ☐ To ☐ From Seller	

The Public Reporting Burden for this collection of information is estimated at 35 minutes per response for collecting, reviewing, and reporting the data. This agency may not collect this information, and you are not required to complete this form, unless it displays a currently valid OMB control number. No confidentiality is assured; this disclosure is mandatory. This is designed to provide the parties to a RESPA covered transaction with information during the settlement process.

Previous editions are obsolete   Page 1 of 3   HUD-1

L. Settlement Charges

		Paid From Borrower's Funds at Settlement	Paid From Seller's Funds at Settlement
700. Total Real Estate Broker Fees			
Division of commission (line 700) as follows:			
701. $ to			
702. $ to			
703. Commission paid at settlement			
704.			
800. Items Payable in Connection with Loan			
801. Our origination charge $	(from GFE #1)		
802. Your credit or charge (points) for the specific interest rate chosen $	(from GFE #2)		
803. Your adjusted origination charges	(from GFE A)		
804. Appraisal fee to	(from GFE #3)		
805. Credit report to	(from GFE #3)		
806. Tax service to	(from GFE #3)		
807. Flood certification	(from GFE #3)		
808.			
900. Items Required by Lender to Be Paid in Advance			
901. Daily interest charges from to @ $ /day	(from GFE #10)		
902. Mortgage insurance premium for months to	(from GFE #3)		
903. Homeowner's insurance for years to	(from GFE #11)		
904.			
1000. Reserves Deposited with Lender			
1001. Initial deposit for your escrow account	(from GFE #9)		
1002. Homeowner's insurance months @ $ per month $			
1003. Mortgage insurance months @ $ per month $			
1004. Property taxes months @ $ per month $			
1005. months @ $ per month $			
1006. months @ $ per month $			
1007. Aggregate Adjustment -$			
1100. Title Charges			
1101. Title services and lender's title insurance	(from GFE #4)		
1102. Settlement or closing fee $			
1103. Owner's title insurance	(from GFE #5)		
1104. Lender's title insurance $			
1105. Lender's title policy limit $			
1106. Owner's title policy limit $			
1107. Agent's portion of the total title insurance premium $			
1108. Underwriter's portion of the total title insurance premium $			
1200. Government Recording and Transfer Charges			
1201. Government recording charges	(from GFE #7)		
1202. Deed $ Mortgage $ Releases $			
1203. Transfer taxes	(from GFE #8)		
1204. City/County tax/stamps Deed $ Mortgage $			
1205. State tax/stamps Deed $ Mortgage $			
1206.			
1300. Additional Settlement Charges			
1301. Required services that you can shop for	(from GFE #6)		
1302. $			
1303. $			
1304.			
1305.			
1400. Total Settlement Charges (enter on lines 103, Section J and 502, Section K)			

Exhibit 13: Settlement Statement (HUD-1): 2 of 3

Comparison of Good Faith Estimate (GFE) and HUD-1 Charges		Good Faith Estimate	HUD-1
Charges That Cannot Increase	**HUD-1 Line Number**		
Our origination charge	# 801		
Your credit or charge (points) for the specific interest rate chosen	# 802		
Your adjusted origination charges	# 803		
Transfer taxes	#1203		

Charges That in Total Cannot Increase More Than 10%		Good Faith Estimate	HUD-1
Government recording charges	# 1201		
	#		
	#		
	#		
	#		
	#		
	#		
	#		
Total			
Increase between GFE and HUD-1 Charges		$ or	%

Charges That Can Change		Good Faith Estimate	HUD-1
Initial deposit for your escrow account	#1001		
Daily interest charges	# 901 $ /day		
Homeowner's insurance	# 903		
	#		
	#		
	#		

Loan Terms

Your initial loan amount is	$
Your loan term is	years
Your initial interest rate is	%
Your initial monthly amount owed for principal, interest, and and any mortgage insurance is	$ includes ☐ Principal ☐ Interest ☐ Mortgage Insurance
Can your interest rate rise?	☐ No. ☐ Yes, it can rise to a maximum of %. The first change will be on and can change again every after . Every change date, your interest rate can increase or decrease by %. Over the life of the loan, your interest rate is guaranteed to never be **lower** than % or **higher** than %.
Even if you make payments on time, can your loan balance rise?	☐ No. ☐ Yes, it can rise to a maximum of $.
Even if you make payments on time, can your monthly amount owed for principal, interest, and mortgage insurance rise?	☐ No. ☐ Yes, the first increase can be on and the monthly amount owed can rise to $. The maximum it can ever rise to is $.
Does your loan have a prepayment penalty?	☐ No. ☐ Yes, your maximum prepayment penalty is $.
Does your loan have a balloon payment?	☐ No. ☐ Yes, you have a balloon payment of $ due in years on .
Total monthly amount owed including escrow account payments	☐ You do not have a monthly escrow payment for items, such as property taxes and homeowner's insurance. You must pay these items directly yourself. ☐ You have an additional monthly escrow payment of $ that results in a total initial monthly amount owed of $. This includes principal, interest, any mortgage insurance and any items checked below: ☐ Property taxes ☐ Homeowner's insurance ☐ Flood insurance ☐ ☐ ☐

Note: If you have any questions about the Settlement Charges and Loan Terms listed on this form, please contact your lender.

Good Faith Estimate (GFE)

Name of Originator		Borrower	
Originator Address			
		Property Address	
Originator Phone Number			
Originator Email		Date of GFE	

Purpose

This GFE gives you an estimate of your settlement charges and loan terms if you are approved for this loan. For more information, see HUD's *Special Information Booklet* on settlement charges, your *Truth-in-Lending Disclosures,* and other consumer information at www.hud.gov/respa. If you decide you would like to proceed with this loan, contact us.

Shopping for your loan

Only you can shop for the best loan for you. Compare this GFE with other loan offers, so you can find the best loan. Use the shopping chart on page 3 to compare all the offers you receive.

Important dates

1. The interest rate for this GFE is available through [＿＿＿＿＿＿＿＿]. After this time, the interest rate, some of your loan Origination Charges, and the monthly payment shown below can change until you lock your interest rate.

2. This estimate for all other settlement charges is available through [＿＿＿＿＿＿＿＿]

3. After you lock your interest rate, you must go to settlement within [＿＿＿＿＿＿＿＿] days (your rate lock period) to receive the locked interest rate.

4. You must lock the interest rate at least [＿＿＿＿＿＿＿＿] days before settlement.

Summary of your loan

Your initial loan amount is	$
Your loan term is	years
Your initial interest rate is	%
Your initial monthly amount owed for principal, interest, and any mortgage insurance is	$ per month
Can your interest rate rise?	☐ No ☐ Yes, it can rise to a maximum of %. The first change will be in
Even if you make payments on time, can your loan balance rise?	☐ No ☐ Yes, it can rise to a maximum of $
Even if you make payments on time, can your monthly amount owed for principal, interest, and any mortgage insurance rise?	☐ No ☐ Yes, the first increase can be in and the monthly amount owed can rise to $. The maximum it can ever rise to is $.
Does your loan have a prepayment penalty?	☐ No ☐ Yes, your maximum prepayment penalty is $
Does your loan have a balloon payment?	☐ No ☐ Yes, you have a balloon payment of $ due in years.

Escrow account information

Some lenders require an escrow account to hold funds for paying property taxes or other property-related charges in addition to your monthly amount owed of $ [＿＿＿＿＿＿].
Do we require you to have an escrow account for your loan?
☐ No, you do not have an escrow account. You must pay these charges directly when due.
☐ Yes, you have an escrow account. It may or may not cover all of these charges. Ask us.

Summary of your settlement charges

A	Your Adjusted Origination Charges (See page 2.)	
B	Your Charges for All Other Settlement Services (See page 2.)	
A + B	Total Estimated Settlement Charges	$

Good Faith Estimate (HUD-GFE) 1

Understanding your estimated settlement charges

Your Adjusted Origination Charges	
1. **Our origination charge** This charge is for getting this loan for you.	
2. **Your credit or charge (points) for the specific interest rate chosen** ☐ The credit or charge for the interest rate of [ ] % is included in "Our origination charge." (See item 1 above.) ☐ You receive a credit of $ [ ] for this interest rate of [ ] %. This credit **reduces** your settlement charges. ☐ You pay a charge of $ [ ] for this interest rate of [ ] %. This charge (points) **increases** your total settlement charges. The tradeoff table on page 3 shows that you can change your total settlement charges by choosing a different interest rate for this loan.	
A Your Adjusted Origination Charges	$

Some of these charges can change at settlement. See the top of page 3 for more information.

Your Charges for All Other Settlement Services	
3. **Required services that we select** These charges are for services we require to complete your settlement. We will choose the providers of these services. Service Charge	
4. **Title services and lender's title insurance** This charge includes the services of a title or settlement agent, for example, and title insurance to protect the lender, if required.	
5. **Owner's title insurance** You may purchase an owner's title insurance policy to protect your interest in the property.	
6. **Required services that you can shop for** These charges are for other services that are required to complete your settlement. We can identify providers of these services or you can shop for them yourself. Our estimates for providing these services are below. Service Charge	
7. **Government recording charges** These charges are for state and local fees to record your loan and title documents.	
8. **Transfer taxes** These charges are for state and local fees on mortgages and home sales.	
9. **Initial deposit for your escrow account** This charge is held in an escrow account to pay future recurring charges on your property and includes ☐ all property taxes, ☐ all insurance, and ☐ other [ ] .	
10. **Daily interest charges** This charge is for the daily interest on your loan from the day of your settlement until the first day of the next month or the first day of your normal mortgage payment cycle. This amount is $ [ ] per day for [ ] days (if your settlement is [ ]).	
11. **Homeowner's insurance** This charge is for the insurance you must buy for the property to protect from a loss, such as fire. Policy Charge	
B Your Charges for All Other Settlement Services	$
A + **B** Total Estimated Settlement Charges	$

Good Faith Estimate (HUD-GFE) 2

Instructions

Understanding which charges can change at settlement

This GFE estimates your settlement charges. At your settlement, you will receive a HUD-1, a form that lists your actual costs. Compare the charges on the HUD-1 with the charges on this GFE. Charges can change if you select your own provider and do not use the companies we identify. (See below for details.)

These charges **cannot increase** at settlement:	The total of these charges **can increase up to 10%** at settlement:	These charges **can change** at settlement:
■ Our origination charge ■ Your credit or charge (points) for the specific interest rate chosen *(after you lock in your interest rate)* ■ Your adjusted origination charges *(after you lock in your interest rate)* ■ Transfer taxes	■ Required services that we select ■ Title services and lender's title insurance *(if we select them or you use companies we identify)* ■ Owner's title insurance *(if you use companies we identify)* ■ Required services that you can shop for *(if you use companies we identify)* ■ Government recording charges	■ Required services that you can shop for (if you do not use companies we identify) ■ Title services and lender's title insurance (if you do not use companies we identify) ■ Owner's title insurance (if you do not use companies we identify) ■ Initial deposit for your escrow account ■ Daily interest charges ■ Homeowner's insurance

Using the tradeoff table

In this GFE, we offered you this loan with a particular interest rate and estimated settlement charges. However:

- If you want to choose this same loan with **lower settlement charges**, then you will have a **higher interest rate**.
- If you want to choose this same loan with a **lower interest rate**, then you will have **higher settlement charges**.

If you would like to choose an available option, you must ask us for a new GFE.

Loan originators have the option to complete this table. Please ask for additional information if the table is not completed.

	The loan in this GFE	The same loan with lower settlement charges	The same loan with a lower interest rate
Your initial loan amount	$	$	$
Your initial interest rate [1]	%	%	%
Your initial monthly amount owed	$	$	$
Change in the monthly amount owed from this GFE	No change	You will pay $ **more** every month	You will pay $ **less** every month
Change in the amount you will pay at settlement with this interest rate	No change	Your settlement charges will be **reduced** by $	Your settlement charges will **increase** by $
How much your total estimated settlement charges will be	$	$	$

[1]For an adjustable rate loan, the comparisons above are for the initial interest rate before adjustments are made.

Using the shopping chart

Use this chart to compare GFEs from different loan originators. Fill in the information by using a different column for each GFE you receive. By comparing loan offers, you can shop for the best loan.

	This loan	Loan 2	Loan 3	Loan 4
Loan originator name				
Initial loan amount				
Loan term				
Initial interest rate				
Initial monthly amount owed				
Rate lock period				
Can interest rate rise?				
Can loan balance rise?				
Can monthly amount owed rise?				
Prepayment penalty?				
Balloon payment?				
Total Estimated Settlement Charges				

If your loan is sold in the future

Some lenders may sell your loan after settlement. Any fees lenders receive in the future cannot change the loan you receive or the charges you paid at settlement.

 Good Faith Estimate (HUD-GFE) 3

Student Learning Outcomes for Module 3

Buying

At the completion of this module, students will be able to:

✔ Explain the meaning of a contract/offer to purchase as a legal document.

✔ List common buyer expenses incurred in escrow

✔ State approximate amounts needed for a down payment and closing costs for purchase of a nearby home.

✔ Describe what an escrow calendar is.

CALIFORNIA
ASSOCIATION
OF REALTORS ®

CALIFORNIA
RESIDENTIAL PURCHASE AGREEMENT
AND JOINT ESCROW INSTRUCTIONS
For Use With Single Family Residential Property — Attached or Detached
(C.A.R. Form RPA-CA, Revised 4/10)

Date _____

1. **OFFER:**
    A. **THIS IS AN OFFER FROM** _____ ("Buyer").
    B. **THE REAL PROPERTY TO BE ACQUIRED** is described as _____
        _____, Assessor's Parcel No. _____, situated in
        _____, County of _____, California ("Property").
    C. **THE PURCHASE PRICE** offered is _____
        _____ (Dollars $ _____).
    D. **CLOSE OF ESCROW** shall occur on _____ (date) (or ☐ _____ **Days** After Acceptance).
2. **AGENCY:**
    A. **DISCLOSURE:** Buyer and Seller each acknowledge prior receipt of a "Disclosure Regarding Real Estate Agency Relationships"
        (C.A.R. Form AD).
    B. **POTENTIALLY COMPETING BUYERS AND SELLERS:** Buyer and Seller each acknowledge receipt of a disclosure of the
        possibility of multiple representation by the Broker representing that principal. This disclosure may be part of a listing
        agreement, buyer representation agreement or separate document (C.A.R. Form DA). Buyer understands that Broker
        representing Buyer may also represent other potential buyers, who may consider, make offers on or ultimately acquire the
        Property. Seller understands that Broker representing Seller may also represent other sellers with competing properties of
        interest to this Buyer.
    C. **CONFIRMATION:** The following agency relationships are hereby confirmed for this transaction:
        Listing Agent _____ (Print Firm Name) is the agent of (check one):
        ☐ the Seller exclusively; or ☐ both the Buyer and Seller.
        Selling Agent _____ (Print Firm Name) (if not the same as the Listing
        Agent) is the agent of (check one): ☐ the Buyer exclusively; or ☐ the Seller exclusively; or ☐ both the Buyer and Seller. Real
        Estate Brokers are not parties to the Agreement between Buyer and Seller.
3. **FINANCE TERMS:** Buyer represents that funds will be good when deposited with Escrow Holder.
    A. **INITIAL DEPOSIT**: Deposit shall be in the amount of . . . .$ _____
        (1) Buyer shall deliver deposit directly to Escrow Holder by personal check, ☐ electronic funds transfer,
        ☐ Other _____ within 3 business days after acceptance
        (or ☐ Other_____);
        OR (2) (If checked) ☐ Buyer has given the deposit by personal check (or to ☐ _____)
        to the agent submitting the offer (or to ☐ _____), made payable to
        _____. The deposit shall be held uncashed until Acceptance and
        then deposited with Escrow Holder (or ☐ into Broker's trust account) within **3 business days** after
        Acceptance (or ☐ Other_____).
    B. **INCREASED DEPOSIT:** Buyer shall deposit with Escrow Holder an increased deposit in the amount of . . . .$ _____
        within _____ **Days** After Acceptance, or ☐ _____.
        If a liquidated damages clause is incorporated into this Agreement, Buyer and Seller shall sign a
        separate liquidated damages clause (C.A.R. Form RID) for any increased deposit at the time it is
        deposited.
    C. **LOAN(S):**
        (1) FIRST LOAN: in the amount of . . . .$ _____
        This loan will be conventional financing or, if checked, ☐ FHA, ☐ VA, ☐ Seller (C.A.R. Form SFA),
        ☐ assumed financing (C.A.R. Form PAA), ☐ Other _____. This loan shall be at a fixed
        rate not to exceed _____% or, ☐ an adjustable rate loan with initial rate not to exceed _____%.
        Regardless of the type of loan, Buyer shall pay points not to exceed _____% of the loan amount.
        (2) ☐ **SECOND LOAN** in the amount of . . . .$ _____
        This loan will be conventional financing or, if checked, ☐ Seller (C.A.R. Form SFA), ☐ assumed
        financing (C.A.R. Form PAA), ☐ Other _____. This loan shall be at a fixed rate not to
        exceed _____% or, ☐ an adjustable rate loan with initial rate not to exceed _____%. Regardless
        of the type of loan, Buyer shall pay points not to exceed _____% of the loan amount.
        (3) FHA/VA: For any FHA or VA loan specified above, Buyer has **17 (or** ☐ _____**) Days** After
        Acceptance to Deliver to Seller written notice (C.A.R. Form FVA) of any lender-required repairs or
        costs that Buyer requests Seller to pay for or repair. Seller has no obligation to pay for repairs or
        satisfy lender requirements unless otherwise agreed in writing.
    D. **ADDITIONAL FINANCING TERMS:** _____
        _____
    E. **BALANCE OF PURCHASE PRICE OR DOWN PAYMENT** in the amount of . . . .$ _____
        to be deposited with Escrow Holder within sufficient time to close escrow.
    F. **PURCHASE PRICE (TOTAL):** . . . .$ _____

Buyer's Initials (_____)(_____)   Seller's Initials (_____)(_____)

RPA-CA REVISED 4/10 (PAGE 1 OF 8) **Print Date BD Apr 10**

| EQUAL HOUSING OPPORTUNITY |

Reviewed by _____ Date _____

CALIFORNIA RESIDENTIAL PURCHASE AGREEMENT (RPA-CA PAGE 1 OF 8)

Property Address: _____ Date: _____

G. **VERIFICATION OF DOWN PAYMENT AND CLOSING COSTS:** Buyer (or Buyer's lender or loan broker pursuant to 3H(1)) shall, within **7 (or ☐ _____) Days** After Acceptance, Deliver to Seller written verification of Buyer's down payment and closing costs. (If checked, ☐ verification attached.)

H. **LOAN TERMS:**

  (1) **LOAN APPLICATIONS:** Within **7 (or ☐ _____) Days** After Acceptance, Buyer shall Deliver to Seller a letter from lender or loan broker stating that, based on a review of Buyer's written application and credit report, Buyer is prequalified or preapproved for any NEW loan specified in 3C above. (If checked, ☐ letter attached.)

  (2) **LOAN CONTINGENCY:** Buyer shall act diligently and in good faith to obtain the designated loan(s). Obtaining the loan(s) specified above **is a contingency** of this Agreement unless otherwise agreed in writing. Buyer's contractual obligations to obtain and provide deposit, balance of down payment and closing costs **are not contingencies** of this Agreement.

  (3) **LOAN CONTINGENCY REMOVAL:**

    (i) Within **17 (or ☐ _____) Days** After Acceptance, Buyer shall, as specified in paragraph 14, in writing remove the loan contingency or cancel this Agreement;

  OR (ii) (If checked) ☐ the loan contingency shall remain in effect until the designated loans are funded.

  (4) ☐ **NO LOAN CONTINGENCY** (If checked): Obtaining any loan specified above is NOT a contingency of this Agreement. If Buyer does not obtain the loan and as a result Buyer does not purchase the Property, Seller may be entitled to Buyer's deposit or other legal remedies.

I. **APPRAISAL CONTINGENCY AND REMOVAL:** This Agreement is (**or,** if checked, ☐ is NOT) contingent upon a written appraisal of the Property by a licensed or certified appraiser at no less than the specified purchase price. If there is a loan contingency, Buyer's removal of the loan contingency shall be deemed removal of this appraisal contingency (**or,** ☐ if checked, Buyer shall, as specified in paragraph 14B(3), in writing remove the appraisal contingency or cancel this Agreement within **17 (or ____) Days** After Acceptance). If there is no loan contingency, Buyer shall, as specified in paragraph 14B(3), in writing remove the appraisal contingency or cancel this Agreement within **17 (or ____) Days** After Acceptance.

J. ☐ **ALL CASH OFFER** (If checked)**:** Buyer shall, within **7 (or ☐ _____) Days** After Acceptance, Deliver to Seller written verification of sufficient funds to close this transaction. (If checked, ☐ verification attached.)

K. **BUYER STATED FINANCING:** Seller has relied on Buyer's representation of the type of financing specified (including but not limited to, as applicable, amount of down payment, contingent or non contingent loan, or all cash). If Buyer seeks alternate financing, (i) Seller has no obligation to cooperate with Buyer's efforts to obtain such financing, and (ii) Buyer shall also pursue the financing method specified in this Agreement. Buyer's failure to secure alternate financing does not excuse Buyer from the obligation to purchase the Property and close escrow as specified in this Agreement.

4. **ALLOCATION OF COSTS** (If checked): Unless otherwise specified in writing, **this paragraph** only determines who is to pay for the inspection, test or service ("Report") mentioned; it **does not determine who is to pay for any work recommended or identified in the Report.**

A. **INSPECTIONS AND REPORTS:**

  (1) ☐ Buyer ☐ Seller shall pay for an inspection and report for wood destroying pests and organisms ("Wood Pest Report") prepared by _____ a registered structural pest control company.

  (2) ☐ Buyer ☐ Seller shall pay to have septic or private sewage disposal systems inspected _____.

  (3) ☐ Buyer ☐ Seller shall pay to have domestic wells tested for water potability and productivity _____.

  (4) ☐ Buyer ☐ Seller shall pay for a natural hazard zone disclosure report prepared by _____.

  (5) ☐ Buyer ☐ Seller shall pay for the following inspection or report _____.

  (6) ☐ Buyer ☐ Seller shall pay for the following inspection or report _____.

B. **GOVERNMENT REQUIREMENTS AND RETROFIT:**

  (1) ☐ Buyer ☐ Seller shall pay for smoke detector installation and/or water heater bracing, if required by Law. Prior to Close Of Escrow, Seller shall provide Buyer written statement(s) of compliance in accordance with state and local Law, unless exempt.

  (2) ☐ Buyer ☐ Seller shall pay the cost of compliance with any other minimum mandatory government retrofit standards, inspections and reports if required as a condition of closing escrow under any Law. _____.

C. **ESCROW AND TITLE:**

  (1) ☐ Buyer ☐ Seller shall pay escrow fee _____.

    Escrow Holder shall be _____.

  (2) ☐ Buyer ☐ Seller shall pay for **owner's** title insurance policy specified in paragraph 12E _____.

    Owner's title policy to be issued by _____.

    (Buyer shall pay for any title insurance policy insuring Buyer's **lender**, unless otherwise agreed in writing.)

D. **OTHER COSTS:**

  (1) ☐ Buyer ☐ Seller shall pay County transfer tax or fee _____.

  (2) ☐ Buyer ☐ Seller shall pay City transfer tax or fee _____.

  (3) ☐ Buyer ☐ Seller shall pay Homeowners' Association ("HOA") transfer fee _____.

  (4) ☐ Buyer ☐ Seller shall pay HOA document preparation fees _____.

  (5) ☐ Buyer ☐ Seller shall pay for any private transfer fee _____.

  (6) ☐ Buyer ☐ Seller shall pay for the cost, not to exceed $ _____, of a one-year home warranty plan, issued by _____, with the following optional coverages:

    ☐ Air Conditioner ☐ Pool/Spa ☐ Code and Permit upgrade ☐ Other: _____

    Buyer is informed that home warranty plans have many optional coverages in addition to those listed above. Buyer is advised to investigate these coverages to determine those that may be suitable for Buyer.

  (7) ☐ Buyer ☐ Seller shall pay for _____.

  (8) ☐ Buyer ☐ Seller shall pay for _____.

Buyer's Initials (_____)(_____)

RPA-CA REVISED 4/10 (PAGE 2 OF 8)

Seller's Initials (_____)(_____)

Reviewed by _____ Date _____

EQUAL HOUSING OPPORTUNITY

CALIFORNIA RESIDENTIAL PURCHASE AGREEMENT (RPA-CA PAGE 2 OF 8)

Property Address: _____ Date: _____

5. CLOSING AND POSSESSION:
  A. Buyer intends (or ☐ does not intend) to occupy the Property as Buyer's primary residence.
  B. Seller-occupied or vacant property: Possession shall be delivered to Buyer at 5 PM or (☐ _____ ☐ AM/☐ PM), on the date of Close Of Escrow; ☐ on _____; or ☐ no later than _____ **Days** After Close Of Escrow. If transfer of title and possession do not occur at the same time, Buyer and Seller are advised to: **(i)** enter into a written occupancy agreement (C.A.R. Form PAA, paragraph 2); and **(ii)** consult with their insurance and legal advisors.
  C. Tenant-occupied property:
      (i) Property shall be vacant at least 5 (or ☐ _____) **Days** Prior to Close Of Escrow, unless otherwise agreed in writing.
      Note to Seller: If you are unable to deliver Property vacant in accordance with rent control and other applicable Law, you may be in breach of this Agreement.
      OR (ii) (if checked) ☐ **Tenant to remain in possession.** (C.A.R. Form PAA, paragraph 3)
  D. At Close Of Escrow, **(i)** Seller assigns to Buyer any assignable warranty rights for items included in the sale, and **(ii)** Seller shall Deliver to Buyer available Copies of warranties. Brokers cannot and will not determine the assignability of any warranties.
  E. At Close Of Escrow, unless otherwise agreed in writing, Seller shall provide keys and/or means to operate all locks, mailboxes, security systems, alarms and garage door openers. If Property is a condominium or located in a common interest subdivision, Buyer may be required to pay a deposit to the Homeowners' Association ("HOA") to obtain keys to accessible HOA facilities.

6. STATUTORY DISCLOSURES (INCLUDING LEAD-BASED PAINT HAZARD DISCLOSURES) AND CANCELLATION RIGHTS:
  A. (1) Seller shall, within the time specified in paragraph 14A, Deliver to Buyer, if required by Law: **(i)** Federal Lead-Based Paint Disclosures (C.A.R. Form FLD) and pamphlet ("Lead Disclosures"); and **(ii)** disclosures or notices required by sections 1102 et. seq. and 1103 et. seq. of the Civil Code ("Statutory Disclosures"). Statutory Disclosures include, but are not limited to, a Real Estate Transfer Disclosure Statement ("TDS"), Natural Hazard Disclosure Statement ("NHD"), notice or actual knowledge of release of illegal controlled substance, notice of special tax and/or assessments (or, if allowed, substantially equivalent notice regarding the Mello-Roos Community Facilities Act and Improvement Bond Act of 1915) and, if Seller has actual knowledge, of industrial use and military ordnance location (C.A.R. Form SPQ or SSD).
      (2) Buyer shall, within the time specified in paragraph 14B(1), return Signed Copies of the Statutory and Lead Disclosures to Seller.
      (3) In the event Seller, prior to Close Of Escrow, becomes aware of adverse conditions materially affecting the Property, or any material inaccuracy in disclosures, information or representations previously provided to Buyer, Seller shall promptly provide a subsequent or amended disclosure or notice, in writing, covering those items. **However, a subsequent or amended disclosure shall not be required for conditions and material inaccuracies** of which Buyer is otherwise aware, or which are **disclosed in reports provided to or obtained by Buyer or ordered and paid for by Buyer.**
      (4) If any disclosure or notice specified in 6A(1), or subsequent or amended disclosure or notice is Delivered to Buyer after the offer is Signed, Buyer shall have the right to cancel this Agreement within **3 Days** After Delivery in person, or **5 Days** After Delivery by deposit in the mail, by giving written notice of cancellation to Seller or Seller's agent.
      (5) Note to Buyer and Seller: Waiver of Statutory and Lead Disclosures is prohibited by Law.
  B. NATURAL AND ENVIRONMENTAL HAZARDS: Within the time specified in paragraph 14A, Seller shall, if required by Law: **(i)** Deliver to Buyer earthquake guides (and questionnaire) and environmental hazards booklet; **(ii)** even if exempt from the obligation to provide a NHD, disclose if the Property is located in a Special Flood Hazard Area; Potential Flooding (Inundation) Area; Very High Fire Hazard Zone; State Fire Responsibility Area; Earthquake Fault Zone; Seismic Hazard Zone; and **(iii)** disclose any other zone as required by Law and provide any other information required for those zones.
  C. WITHHOLDING TAXES: Within the time specified in paragraph 14A, to avoid required withholding, Seller shall Deliver to Buyer or qualified substitute, an affidavit sufficient to comply with federal (FIRPTA) and California withholding Law (C.A.R. Form AS or QS).
  D. MEGAN'S LAW DATABASE DISCLOSURE: Notice: Pursuant to Section 290.46 of the Penal Code, information about specified registered sex offenders is made available to the public via an Internet Web site maintained by the Department of Justice at www.meganslaw.ca.gov. Depending on an offender's criminal history, this information will include either the address at which the offender resides or the community of residence and ZIP Code in which he or she resides. (Neither Seller nor Brokers are required to check this website. If Buyer wants further information, Broker recommends that Buyer obtain information from this website during Buyer's inspection contingency period. Brokers do not have expertise in this area.)

7. CONDOMINIUM/PLANNED DEVELOPMENT DISCLOSURES:
  A. SELLER HAS: 7 (or ☐ _____**) Days** After Acceptance to disclose to Buyer whether the Property is a condominium, or is located in a planned development or other common interest subdivision (C.A.R. Form SPQ or SSD).
  B. If the Property is a condominium or is located in a planned development or other common interest subdivision, Seller has **3 (or** ☐ _____**) Days** After Acceptance to request from the HOA (C.A.R. Form HOA): **(i)** Copies of any documents required by Law; **(ii)** disclosure of any pending or anticipated claim or litigation by or against the HOA; **(iii)** a statement containing the location and number of designated parking and storage spaces; **(iv)** Copies of the most recent 12 months of HOA minutes for regular and special meetings; and **(v)** the names and contact information of all HOAs governing the Property (collectively, "CI Disclosures"). Seller shall itemize and Deliver to Buyer all CI Disclosures received from the HOA and any CI Disclosures in Seller's possession. Buyer's approval of CI Disclosures is a contingency of this Agreement as specified in paragraph 14B(3).

8. ITEMS INCLUDED IN AND EXCLUDED FROM PURCHASE PRICE:
  A. NOTE TO BUYER AND SELLER: Items listed as included or excluded in the MLS, flyers or marketing materials are **not** included in the purchase price or excluded from the sale unless specified in 8B or C.
  B. ITEMS INCLUDED IN SALE:
      (1) All EXISTING fixtures and fittings that are attached to the Property;
      (2) EXISTING electrical, mechanical, lighting, plumbing and heating fixtures, ceiling fans, fireplace inserts, gas logs and grates, solar systems, built-in appliances, window and door screens, awnings, shutters, window coverings, attached floor coverings, television antennas, satellite dishes, private integrated telephone systems, air coolers/conditioners, pool/spa equipment, garage door openers/remote controls, mailbox, in-ground landscaping, trees/shrubs, water softeners, water purifiers, security systems/alarms; (If checked) ☐ stove(s), ☐ refrigerator(s); and
      (3) The following additional items:_____.
      (4) Seller represents that all items included in the purchase price, unless otherwise specified, are owned by Seller.
      (5) All items included shall be transferred free of liens and without Seller warranty.
  C. ITEMS EXCLUDED FROM SALE: Unless otherwise specified, audio and video components (such as flat screen TVs and speakers) are excluded if any such item is not itself attached to the Property, even if a bracket or other mechanism attached to the component is attached to the Property; and _____.

Buyer's Initials (_____)(_____)   Seller's Initials (_____)(_____)

RPA-CA REVISED 4/10 (PAGE 3 OF 8)

Reviewed by _____ Date _____

Property Address: _____ Date: _____

9. **CONDITION OF PROPERTY:** Unless otherwise agreed: **(i) the Property is sold (a) in its PRESENT physical ("as-is") condition as of the date of Acceptance and (b) subject to Buyer's Investigation rights; (ii)** the Property, including pool, spa, landscaping and grounds, is to be maintained in substantially the same condition as of the date of Acceptance; and **(iii)** all debris and personal property not included in the sale shall be removed by Seller by Close Of Escrow.
   A. Seller shall, within the time specified in paragraph 14A, DISCLOSE KNOWN MATERIAL FACTS AND DEFECTS affecting the Property, including known insurance claims within the past five years, and make any and all other disclosures required by law.
   B. Buyer has the right to inspect the Property and, as specified in paragraph 14B, based upon information discovered in those inspections: (i) cancel this Agreement; or (ii) request that Seller make Repairs or take other action.
   C. **Buyer is strongly advised to conduct investigations of the entire Property in order to determine its present condition. Seller may not be aware of all defects affecting the Property or other factors that Buyer considers important. Property improvements may not be built according to code, in compliance with current Law, or have had permits issued.**

10. **BUYER'S INVESTIGATION OF PROPERTY AND MATTERS AFFECTING PROPERTY:**
   A. Buyer's acceptance of the condition of, and any other matter affecting the Property, is a contingency of this Agreement as specified in this paragraph and paragraph 14B. Within the time specified in paragraph 14B(1), Buyer shall have the right, at Buyer's expense unless otherwise agreed, to conduct inspections, investigations, tests, surveys and other studies ("Buyer Investigations"), including, but not limited to, the right to: **(i)** inspect for lead-based paint and other lead-based paint hazards; **(ii)** inspect for wood destroying pests and organisms; **(iii)** review the registered sex offender database; **(iv)** confirm the insurability of Buyer and the Property; and **(v)** satisfy Buyer as to any matter specified in the attached Buyer's Inspection Advisory (C.A.R. Form BIA). Without Seller's prior written consent, Buyer shall neither make nor cause to be made: **(i)** invasive or destructive Buyer Investigations; or **(ii)** inspections by any governmental building or zoning inspector or government employee, unless required by Law.
   B. Seller shall make the Property available for all Buyer Investigations. Buyer shall **(i)** as specified in paragraph 14B, complete Buyer Investigations and, either remove the contingency or cancel this Agreement, and **(ii)** give Seller, at no cost, complete Copies of all Investigation reports obtained by Buyer, which obligation shall survive the termination of this Agreement.
   C. Seller shall have water, gas, electricity and all operable pilot lights on for Buyer's Investigations and through the date possession is made available to Buyer.
   D. **Buyer indemnity and Seller protection for entry upon property:** Buyer shall: **(i)** keep the Property free and clear of liens; **(ii)** repair all damage arising from Buyer Investigations; and **(iii)** indemnify and hold Seller harmless from all resulting liability, claims, demands, damages and costs of Buyer's Investigations. Buyer shall carry, or Buyer shall require anyone acting on Buyer's behalf to carry, policies of liability, workers' compensation and other applicable insurance, defending and protecting Seller from liability for any injuries to persons or property occurring during any Buyer Investigations or work done on the Property at Buyer's direction prior to Close Of Escrow. Seller is advised that certain protections may be afforded Seller by recording a "Notice of Non-responsibility" (C.A.R. Form NNR) for Buyer Investigations and work done on the Property at Buyer's direction. Buyer's obligations under this paragraph shall survive the termination or cancellation of this Agreement and Close Of Escrow.

11. **SELLER DISCLOSURES; ADDENDA; ADVISORIES; OTHER TERMS:**
   A. **Seller Disclosures (if checked):** Seller shall, within the time specified in paragraph 14A, complete and provide Buyer with a:
      ☐ Seller Property Questionnaire (C.A.R. Form SPQ) **OR** ☐ Supplemental Contractual and Statutory Disclosure (C.A.R. Form SSD)
   B. **Addenda (if checked):** ☐ Addendum # _____ (C.A.R. Form ADM)
      ☐ Wood Destroying Pest Inspection and Allocation of Cost Addendum (C.A.R. Form WPA)
      ☐ Purchase Agreement Addendum (C.A.R. Form PAA)   ☐ Septic, Well and Property Monument Addendum (C.A.R. Form SWPI)
      ☐ Short Sale Addendum (C.A.R. Form SSA)   ☐ Other
   C. **Advisories (If checked):**   ☑ Buyer's Inspection Advisory (C.A.R. Form BIA)
      ☐ Probate Advisory (C.A.R. Form PAK)   ☐ Statewide Buyer and Seller Advisory (C.A.R. Form SBSA)
      ☐ Trust Advisory (C.A.R. Form TA)   ☐ REO Advisory (C.A.R. Form REO)
   D. **Other Terms**:

12. **TITLE AND VESTING:**
   A. Within the time specified in paragraph 14, Buyer shall be provided a current preliminary title report, which shall include a search of the General Index. Seller shall within 7 Days After Acceptance give Escrow Holder a completed Statement of Information. The preliminary report is only an offer by the title insurer to issue a policy of title insurance and may not contain every item affecting title. Buyer's review of the preliminary report and any other matters which may affect title are a contingency of this Agreement as specified in paragraph 14B.
   B. Title is taken in its present condition subject to all encumbrances, easements, covenants, conditions, restrictions, rights and other matters, whether of record or not, as of the date of Acceptance except: **(i)** monetary liens of record unless Buyer is assuming those obligations or taking the Property subject to those obligations; and **(ii)** those matters which Seller has agreed to remove in writing.
   C. Within the time specified in paragraph 14A, Seller has a duty to disclose to Buyer all matters known to Seller affecting title, whether of record or not.
   D. At Close Of Escrow, Buyer shall receive a grant deed conveying title (or, for stock cooperative or long-term lease, an assignment of stock certificate or of Seller's leasehold interest), including oil, mineral and water rights if currently owned by Seller. Title shall vest as designated in Buyer's supplemental escrow instructions. THE MANNER OF TAKING TITLE MAY HAVE SIGNIFICANT LEGAL AND TAX CONSEQUENCES. CONSULT AN APPROPRIATE PROFESSIONAL.
   E. Buyer shall receive a CLTA/ALTA Homeowner's Policy of Title Insurance. A title company, at Buyer's request, can provide information about the availability, desirability, coverage, survey requirements, and cost of various title insurance coverages and endorsements. If Buyer desires title coverage other than that required by this paragraph, Buyer shall instruct Escrow Holder in writing and pay any increase in cost.

13. **SALE OF BUYER'S PROPERTY:**
   A. This Agreement is NOT contingent upon the sale of any property owned by Buyer.
   OR B. ☐ (If checked): The attached addendum (C.A.R. Form COP) regarding the contingency for the sale of property owned by Buyer is incorporated into this Agreement.

Seller's Initials (_____)(_____)

Copyright © 1991-2010, CALIFORNIA ASSOCIATION OF REALTORS®, INC.

| Reviewed by _____ Date _____ |

RPA-CA REVISED 4/10 (PAGE 4 OF 8)

CALIFORNIA RESIDENTIAL PURCHASE AGREEMENT (RPA-CA PAGE 4 OF 8)

Property Address: _____ Date: _____

14. **TIME PERIODS; REMOVAL OF CONTINGENCIES; CANCELLATION RIGHTS:** The following time periods may only be extended, altered, modified or changed by mutual written agreement. Any removal of contingencies or cancellation under this paragraph by either Buyer or Seller must be exercised in good faith and in writing (C.A.R. Form CR or CC).

   A. SELLER HAS: 7 (or ☐ _____) Days After Acceptance to Deliver to Buyer all Reports, disclosures and information for which Seller is responsible under paragraphs 4, 6A, B and C, 7A, 9A, 11A and B, and 12. Buyer may give Seller a Notice to Seller to Perform (C.A.R. Form NSP) if Seller has not Delivered the items within the time specified.

   B. **(1) BUYER HAS: 17 (or ☐ _____) Days** After Acceptance, unless otherwise agreed in writing, to:

      (i) complete all Buyer Investigations; approve all disclosures, reports and other applicable information, which Buyer receives from Seller; and approve all other matters affecting the Property; and

      (ii) Deliver to Seller Signed Copies of Statutory and Lead Disclosures Delivered by Seller in accordance with paragraph 6A.

    (2) Within the time specified in 14B(1), Buyer may request that Seller make repairs or take any other action regarding the Property (C.A.R. Form RR). Seller has no obligation to agree to or respond to Buyer's requests.

    (3) Within the time specified in 14B(1) (or as otherwise specified in this Agreement), Buyer shall Deliver to Seller either (i) a removal of the applicable contingency (C.A.R. Form CR), or (ii) a cancellation (C.A.R. Form CC) of this Agreement based upon a remaining contingency or Seller's failure to Deliver the specified items. However, if any report, disclosure or information for which Seller is responsible is not Delivered within the time specified in 14A, then Buyer has **5 (or ☐ _____) Days** After Delivery of any such items, or the time specified in 14B(1), whichever is later, to Deliver to Seller a removal of the applicable contingency or cancellation of this Agreement.

    (4) Continuation of Contingency: Even after the end of the time specified in 14B(1) and before Seller cancels this Agreement, if at all, pursuant to 14C, Buyer retains the right to either (i) in writing remove remaining contingencies, or (ii) cancel this Agreement based upon a remaining contingency or Seller's failure to Deliver the specified items. Once Buyer's written removal of all contingencies is Delivered to Seller, Seller may not cancel this Agreement pursuant to 14C(1).

   C. SELLER RIGHT TO CANCEL:

    (1) Seller right to Cancel; Buyer Contingencies: If, within time specified in this Agreement, Buyer does not, in writing, Deliver to Seller a removal of the applicable contingency or cancellation of this Agreement then Seller, after first Delivering to Buyer a Notice to Buyer to Perform (C.A.R. Form NBP) may cancel this Agreement. In such event, Seller shall authorize return of Buyer's deposit.

    (2) Seller right to Cancel; Buyer Contract Obligations: Seller, after first Delivering to Buyer a NBP may cancel this Agreement for any of the following reasons: **(i)** if Buyer fails to deposit funds as required by 3A or 3B; **(ii)** if the funds deposited pursuant to 3A or 3B are not good when deposited; **(iii)** if Buyer fails to Deliver a notice of FHA or VA costs or terms as required by 3C(3) (C.A.R. Form FVA); **(iv)** if Buyer fails to Deliver a letter as required by 3H; **(v)** if Buyer fails to Deliver verification as required by 3G or 3J; **(vi)** if Seller reasonably disapproves of the verification provided by 3G or 3J; **(vii)** if Buyer fails to return Statutory and Lead Disclosures as required by paragraph 6A(2); or **(viii)** if Buyer fails to sign or initial a separate liquidated damages form for an increased deposit as required by paragraphs 3B and 25. In such event, Seller shall authorize return of Buyer's deposit.

    (3) Notice To Buyer To Perform: The NBP shall: **(i)** be in writing; **(ii)** be signed by Seller; and **(iii)** give Buyer at least **2 (or ☐ _____) Days** After Delivery (or until the time specified in the applicable paragraph, whichever occurs last) to take the applicable action. A NBP may not be Delivered any earlier than **2 Days** Prior to the expiration of the applicable time for Buyer to remove a contingency or cancel this Agreement or meet an obligation specified in 14C(2).

   D. EFFECT OF BUYER'S REMOVAL OF CONTINGENCIES: If Buyer removes, in writing, any contingency or cancellation rights, unless otherwise specified in a separate written agreement between Buyer and Seller, Buyer shall with regard to that contingency or cancellation right conclusively be deemed to have: **(i)** completed all Buyer Investigations, and review of reports and other applicable information and disclosures; **(ii)** elected to proceed with the transaction; and **(iii)** assumed all liability, responsibility and expense for Repairs or corrections or for inability to obtain financing.

   E. CLOSE OF ESCROW: Before Seller or Buyer may cancel this Agreement for failure of the other party to close escrow pursuant to this Agreement, Seller or Buyer must first Deliver to the other a demand to close escrow (C.A.R. Form DCE).

   F. EFFECT OF CANCELLATION ON DEPOSITS: If Buyer or Seller gives written notice of cancellation pursuant to rights duly exercised under the terms of this Agreement, Buyer and Seller agree to Sign mutual instructions to cancel the sale and escrow and release deposits, if any, to the party entitled to the funds, less fees and costs incurred by that party. Fees and costs may be payable to service providers and vendors for services and products provided during escrow. **Release of funds will require mutual Signed release instructions from Buyer and Seller, judicial decision or arbitration award. A Buyer or Seller may be subject to a civil penalty of up to $1,000 for refusal to sign such instructions if no good faith dispute exists as to who is entitled to the deposited funds (Civil Code §1057.3).**

15. **REPAIRS:** Repairs shall be completed prior to final verification of condition unless otherwise agreed in writing. Repairs to be performed at Seller's expense may be performed by Seller or through others, provided that the work complies with applicable Law, including governmental permit, inspection and approval requirements. Repairs shall be performed in a good, skillful manner with materials of quality and appearance comparable to existing materials. It is understood that exact restoration of appearance or cosmetic items following all Repairs may not be possible. Seller shall: **(i)** obtain receipts for Repairs performed by others; **(ii)** prepare a written statement indicating the Repairs performed by Seller and the date of such Repairs; and **(iii)** provide Copies of receipts and statements to Buyer prior to final verification of condition.

16. **FINAL VERIFICATION OF CONDITION:** Buyer shall have the right to make a final inspection of the Property within **5 (or _____) Days** Prior to Close Of Escrow, NOT AS A CONTINGENCY OF THE SALE, but solely to confirm: **(i)** the Property is maintained pursuant to paragraph 9; **(ii)** Repairs have been completed as agreed; and **(iii)** Seller has complied with Seller's other obligations under this Agreement (C.A.R. Form VP).

17. **PRORATIONS OF PROPERTY TAXES AND OTHER ITEMS:** Unless otherwise agreed in writing, the following items shall be PAID CURRENT and prorated between Buyer and Seller as of Close Of Escrow: real property taxes and assessments, interest, rents, HOA regular, special, and emergency dues and assessments imposed prior to Close Of Escrow, premiums on insurance assumed by Buyer, payments on bonds and assessments assumed by Buyer, and payments on Mello-Roos and other Special Assessment District bonds and assessments that are a current lien. The following items shall be assumed by Buyer WITHOUT CREDIT toward the purchase price: prorated payments on Mello-Roos and other Special Assessment District bonds and assessments and HOA special assessments that are a current lien but not yet due. Property will be reassessed upon change of ownership. Any supplemental tax bills shall be paid as follows: **(i)** for periods after Close Of Escrow, by Buyer; and **(ii)** for periods prior to Close Of Escrow, by Seller (see C.A.R. Form SPT or SBSA for further information). TAX BILLS ISSUED AFTER CLOSE OF ESCROW SHALL BE HANDLED DIRECTLY BETWEEN BUYER AND SELLER. Prorations shall be made based on a 30-day month.

Buyer's Initials (_____)(_____)

RPA-CA REVISED 4/10 (PAGE 5 OF 8)

Seller's Initials (_____)(_____)

Reviewed by _____ Date _____

EQUAL HOUSING OPPORTUNITY

CALIFORNIA RESIDENTIAL PURCHASE AGREEMENT (RPA-CA PAGE 5 OF 8)

Property Address: _____ Date: _____

18. SELECTION OF SERVICE PROVIDERS: Brokers do not guarantee the performance of any vendors, service or product providers ("Providers"), whether referred by Broker or selected by Buyer, Seller or other person. Buyer and Seller may select ANY Providers of their own choosing.

19. MULTIPLE LISTING SERVICE ("MLS"): Brokers are authorized to report to the MLS a pending sale and, upon Close Of Escrow, the sales price and other terms of this transaction shall be provided to the MLS to be published and disseminated to persons and entities authorized to use the information on terms approved by the MLS.

20. EQUAL HOUSING OPPORTUNITY: The Property is sold in compliance with federal, state and local anti-discrimination Laws.

21. ATTORNEY FEES: In any action, proceeding, or arbitration between Buyer and Seller arising out of this Agreement, the prevailing Buyer or Seller shall be entitled to reasonable attorney fees and costs from the non-prevailing Buyer or Seller, except as provided in paragraph 26A.

22. DEFINITIONS: As used in this Agreement:
   A. **"Acceptance"** means the time the offer or final counter offer is accepted in writing by a party and is delivered to and personally received by the other party or that party's authorized agent in accordance with the terms of this offer or a final counter offer.
   B. **"C.A.R. Form"** means the specific form referenced or another comparable form agreed to by the parties.
   C. **"Close Of Escrow"** means the date the grant deed, or other evidence of transfer of title, is recorded.
   D. **"Copy"** means copy by any means including photocopy, NCR, facsimile and electronic.
   E. **"Days"** means calendar days. However, after Acceptance, the last **Day** for performance of any act required by this Agreement (including Close Of Escrow) shall not include any Saturday, Sunday, or legal holiday and shall instead be the next Day.
   F. **"Days After"** means the specified number of calendar days after the occurrence of the event specified, not counting the calendar date on which the specified event occurs, and ending at 11:59 PM on the final day.
   G. **"Days Prior"** means the specified number of calendar days before the occurrence of the event specified, not counting the calendar date on which the specified event is scheduled to occur.
   H. **"Deliver"**, **"Delivered"** or **"Delivery"**, regardless of the method used (i.e. messenger, mail, email, fax, other), means and shall be effective upon (i) personal receipt by Buyer or Seller or the individual Real Estate Licensee for that principal as specified in paragraph D of the section titled Real Estate Brokers on page 8;
   OR (ii) if checked, ☐ per the attached addendum (C.A.R. Form RDN).
   I. **"Electronic Copy"** or **"Electronic Signature"** means, as applicable, an electronic copy or signature complying with California Law. Buyer and Seller agree that electronic means will not be used by either party to modify or alter the content or integrity of this Agreement without the knowledge and consent of the other party.
   J. **"Law"** means any law, code, statute, ordinance, regulation, rule or order, which is adopted by a controlling city, county, state or federal legislative, judicial or executive body or agency.
   K. **"Repairs"** means any repairs (including pest control), alterations, replacements, modifications or retrofitting of the Property provided for under this Agreement.
   L. **"Signed"** means either a handwritten or electronic signature on an original document, Copy or any counterpart.

23. BROKER COMPENSATION: Seller or Buyer, or both, as applicable, agree(s) to pay compensation to Broker as specified in a separate written agreement between Broker and that Seller or Buyer. Compensation is payable upon Close Of Escrow, or if escrow does not close, as otherwise specified in the agreement between Broker and that Seller or Buyer.

24. JOINT ESCROW INSTRUCTIONS TO ESCROW HOLDER:
   A. **The following paragraphs, or applicable portions thereof, of this Agreement constitute the joint escrow instructions of Buyer and Seller to Escrow Holder,** which Escrow Holder is to use along with any related counter offers and addenda, and any additional mutual instructions to close the escrow: 1, 3, 4, 6C, 11B and D, 12, 13B, 14F, 17, 22, 23, 24, 28, 30, and paragraph D of the section titled Real Estate Brokers on page 8. If a Copy of the separate compensation agreement(s) provided for in paragraph 23, or paragraph D of the section titled Real Estate Brokers on page 8 is deposited with Escrow Holder by Broker, Escrow Holder shall accept such agreement(s) and pay out of Buyer's or Seller's funds, or both, as applicable, the respective Broker's compensation provided for in such agreement(s). The terms and conditions of this Agreement not specifically referenced above, in the specified paragraphs are additional matters for the information of Escrow Holder, but about which Escrow Holder need not be concerned. Buyer and Seller will receive Escrow Holder's general provisions directly from Escrow Holder and will execute such provisions upon Escrow Holder's request. To the extent the general provisions are inconsistent or conflict with this Agreement, the general provisions will control as to the duties and obligations of Escrow Holder only. Buyer and Seller will execute additional instructions, documents and forms provided by Escrow Holder that are reasonably necessary to close the escrow.
   B. A Copy of this Agreement shall be delivered to Escrow Holder within **3** business days after Acceptance (or ☐ _____). Escrow Holder shall provide Seller's Statement of Information to Title company when received from Seller. Buyer and Seller authorize Escrow Holder to accept and rely on Copies and Signatures as defined in this Agreement as originals, to open escrow and for other purposes of escrow. The validity of this Agreement as between Buyer and Seller is not affected by whether or when Escrow Holder Signs this Agreement.
   C. Brokers are a party to the escrow for the sole purpose of compensation pursuant to paragraph 23 and paragraph D of the section titled Real Estate Brokers on page 8. Buyer and Seller irrevocably assign to Brokers compensation specified in paragraph 23, respectively, and irrevocably instruct Escrow Holder to disburse those funds to Brokers at Close Of Escrow or pursuant to any other mutually executed cancellation agreement. Compensation instructions can be amended or revoked only with the written consent of Brokers. Buyer and Seller shall release and hold harmless Escrow Holder from any liability resulting from Escrow Holder's payment to Broker(s) of compensation pursuant to this Agreement. Escrow Holder shall immediately notify Brokers: **(i)** if Buyer's initial or any additional deposit is not made pursuant to this Agreement, or is not good at time of deposit with Escrow Holder; or **(ii)** if either Buyer or Seller instruct Escrow Holder to cancel escrow.
   D. A Copy of any amendment that affects any paragraph of this Agreement for which Escrow Holder is responsible shall be delivered to Escrow Holder within **2** business days after mutual execution of the amendment.

Buyer's Initials (_____)(_____)   Seller's Initials (_____)(_____)

RPA-CA REVISED 4/10 (PAGE 6 OF 8)

Reviewed by _____ Date _____

EQUAL HOUSING OPPORTUNITY

CALIFORNIA RESIDENTIAL PURCHASE AGREEMENT (RPA-CA PAGE 6 OF 8)

25. **LIQUIDATED DAMAGES:** If Buyer fails to complete this purchase because of Buyer's default, Seller shall retain, as liquidated damages, the deposit actually paid. If the Property is a dwelling with no more than four units, one of which Buyer intends to occupy, then the amount retained shall be no more than 3% of the purchase price. Any excess shall be returned to Buyer. Release of funds will require mutual, Signed release instructions from both Buyer and Seller, judicial decision or arbitration award. AT TIME OF THE INCREASED DEPOSIT BUYER AND SELLER SHALL SIGN A SEPARATE LIQUIDATED DAMAGES PROVISION FOR ANY INCREASED DEPOSIT (C.A.R. FORM RID).

26. **DISPUTE RESOLUTION:**

Buyer's Initials _____/_____	Seller's Initials _____/_____

    A.   **MEDIATION:** Buyer and Seller agree to mediate any dispute or claim arising between them out of this Agreement, or any resulting transaction, before resorting to arbitration or court action. **Buyer and Seller also agree to mediate any disputes or claims with Broker(s) who, in writing, agree to such mediation prior to, or within a reasonable time after, the dispute or claim is presented to the Broker.** Mediation fees, if any, shall be divided equally among the parties involved. If, for any dispute or claim to which this paragraph applies, any party (i) commences an action without first attempting to resolve the matter through mediation, or (ii) before commencement of an action, refuses to mediate after a request has been made, then that party shall not be entitled to recover attorney fees, even if they would otherwise be available to that party in any such action. THIS MEDIATION PROVISION APPLIES WHETHER OR NOT THE ARBITRATION PROVISION IS INITIALED. **Exclusions from this mediation agreement are specified in paragraph 26C.**

    B.   **ARBITRATION OF DISPUTES:**

       Buyer and Seller agree that any dispute or claim in Law or equity arising between them out of this Agreement or any resulting transaction, which is not settled through mediation, shall be decided by neutral, binding arbitration. Buyer and Seller also agree to arbitrate any disputes or claims with Broker(s) who, in writing, agree to such arbitration prior to, or within a reasonable time after, the dispute or claim is presented to the Broker. The arbitrator shall be a retired judge or justice, or an attorney with at least 5 years of residential real estate Law experience, unless the parties mutually agree to a different arbitrator. The parties shall have the right to discovery in accordance with Code of Civil Procedure §1283.05. In all other respects, the arbitration shall be conducted in accordance with Title 9 of Part 3 of the Code of Civil Procedure. Judgment upon the award of the arbitrator(s) may be entered into any court having jurisdiction. Enforcement of this agreement to arbitrate shall be governed by the Federal Arbitration Act. Exclusions from this arbitration agreement are specified in paragraph 26C.

          "NOTICE: BY INITIALING IN THE SPACE BELOW YOU ARE AGREEING TO HAVE ANY DISPUTE ARISING OUT OF THE MATTERS INCLUDED IN THE 'ARBITRATION OF DISPUTES' PROVISION DECIDED BY NEUTRAL ARBITRATION AS PROVIDED BY CALIFORNIA LAW AND YOU ARE GIVING UP ANY RIGHTS YOU MIGHT POSSESS TO HAVE THE DISPUTE LITIGATED IN A COURT OR JURY TRIAL. BY INITIALING IN THE SPACE BELOW YOU ARE GIVING UP YOUR JUDICIAL RIGHTS TO DISCOVERY AND APPEAL, UNLESS THOSE RIGHTS ARE SPECIFICALLY INCLUDED IN THE 'ARBITRATION OF DISPUTES' PROVISION. IF YOU REFUSE TO SUBMIT TO ARBITRATION AFTER AGREEING TO THIS PROVISION, YOU MAY BE COMPELLED TO ARBITRATE UNDER THE AUTHORITY OF THE CALIFORNIA CODE OF CIVIL PROCEDURE. YOUR AGREEMENT TO THIS ARBITRATION PROVISION IS VOLUNTARY."

          "WE HAVE READ AND UNDERSTAND THE FOREGOING AND AGREE TO SUBMIT DISPUTES ARISING OUT OF THE MATTERS INCLUDED IN THE 'ARBITRATION OF DISPUTES' PROVISION TO NEUTRAL ARBITRATION."

Buyer's Initials _____/_____	Seller's Initials _____/_____

    C.   **ADDITIONAL MEDIATION AND ARBITRATION TERMS:**

       (1) **EXCLUSIONS:** The following matters shall be excluded from mediation and arbitration: (i) a judicial or non-judicial foreclosure or other action or proceeding to enforce a deed of trust, mortgage or installment land sale contract as defined in Civil Code §2985; (ii) an unlawful detainer action; (iii) the filing or enforcement of a mechanic's lien; and (iv) any matter that is within the jurisdiction of a probate, small claims or bankruptcy court. The filing of a court action to enable the recording of a notice of pending action, for order of attachment, receivership, injunction, or other provisional remedies, shall not constitute a waiver or violation of the mediation and arbitration provisions.

       (2) **BROKERS:** Brokers shall not be obligated or compelled to mediate or arbitrate unless they agree to do so in writing. Any Broker(s) participating in mediation or arbitration shall not be deemed a party to the Agreement.

27. **TERMS AND CONDITIONS OF OFFER:**

    This is an offer to purchase the Property on the above terms and conditions. The liquidated damages paragraph or the arbitration of disputes paragraph is incorporated in this Agreement if initialed by all parties or if incorporated by mutual agreement in a counter offer or addendum. If at least one but not all parties initial such paragraph(s), a counter offer is required until agreement is reached. Seller has the right to continue to offer the Property for sale and to accept any other offer at any time prior to notification of Acceptance. If this offer is accepted and Buyer subsequently defaults, Buyer may be responsible for payment of Brokers' compensation. This Agreement and any supplement, addendum or modification, including any Copy, may be Signed in two or more counterparts, all of which shall constitute one and the same writing.

28. **TIME OF ESSENCE; ENTIRE CONTRACT; CHANGES:** Time is of the essence. All understandings between the parties are incorporated in this Agreement. Its terms are intended by the parties as a final, complete and exclusive expression of their Agreement with respect to its subject matter, and may not be contradicted by evidence of any prior agreement or contemporaneous oral agreement. If any provision of this Agreement is held to be ineffective or invalid, the remaining provisions will nevertheless be given full force and effect. Except as otherwise specified, this Agreement shall be interpreted and disputes shall be resolved in accordance with the laws of the State of California. **Neither this Agreement nor any provision in it may be extended, amended, modified, altered or changed, except in writing Signed by Buyer and Seller.**

Buyer's Initials (_____)(_____)   Seller's Initials (_____)(_____)

RPA-CA REVISED 4/10 (PAGE 7 OF 8)

Reviewed by _____ Date _____

EQUAL HOUSING OPPORTUNITY

CALIFORNIA RESIDENTIAL PURCHASE AGREEMENT (RPA-CA PAGE 7 OF 8)

Property Address: _____ Date: _____

29. EXPIRATION OF OFFER: This offer shall be deemed revoked and the deposit shall be returned unless the offer is Signed by Seller and a Copy of the Signed offer is personally received by Buyer, or by _____, who is authorized to receive it, by 5:00 PM on the third Day after this offer is signed by Buyer (or, if checked, ☐ by _____ ☐AM/☐PM, on _____(date)).

Buyer has read and acknowledges receipt of a Copy of the offer and agrees to the above confirmation of agency relationships.

Date _____ Date _____
BUYER _____ BUYER _____
_____ _____
(Print name) **(Print name)**
_____
(Address)
☐ Additional Signature Addendum attached (C.A.R. Form ASA).

30. ACCEPTANCE OF OFFER: Seller warrants that Seller is the owner of the Property, or has the authority to execute this Agreement. Seller accepts the above offer, agrees to sell the Property on the above terms and conditions, and agrees to the above confirmation of agency relationships. Seller has read and acknowledges receipt of a Copy of this Agreement, and authorizes Broker to Deliver a Signed Copy to Buyer.
☐ (If checked) **SUBJECT TO ATTACHED COUNTER OFFER (C.A.R. Form CO) DATED:** _____.

Date _____ Date _____
SELLER _____ SELLER _____
_____ _____
(Print name) **(Print name)**
_____
(Address)
☐ Additional Signature Addendum attached (C.A.R. Form ASA).

(____/____) **CONFIRMATION OF ACCEPTANCE:** A Copy of Signed Acceptance was personally received by Buyer or Buyer's
(Initials) authorized agent on (date) _____ at _____ ☐AM/☐PM. **A binding Agreement is created when a Copy of Signed Acceptance is personally received by Buyer or Buyer's authorized agent whether or not confirmed in this document. Completion of this confirmation is not legally required in order to create a binding Agreement. It is solely intended to evidence the date that Confirmation of Acceptance has occurred.**

REAL ESTATE BROKERS:
A. Real Estate Brokers are not parties to the Agreement between Buyer and Seller.
B. Agency relationships are confirmed as stated in paragraph 2.
C. If specified in paragraph 3A(2), Agent who submitted the offer for Buyer acknowledges receipt of deposit.
D. **COOPERATING BROKER COMPENSATION:** Listing Broker agrees to pay Cooperating Broker **(Selling Firm)** and Cooperating Broker agrees to accept, out of Listing Broker's proceeds in escrow: **(i)** the amount specified in the MLS, provided Cooperating Broker is a Participant of the MLS in which the Property is offered for sale or a reciprocal MLS; or **(ii)** ☐ (if checked) the amount specified in a separate written agreement (C.A.R. Form CBC) between Listing Broker and Cooperating Broker. Declaration of License and Tax (C.A.R. Form DLT) may be used to document that tax reporting will be required or that an exemption exists.

Real Estate Broker (Selling Firm) _____ DRE Lic. #_____
By _____ DRE Lic. # _____ Date _____
Address _____ City _____ State _____ Zip _____
Telephone _____ Fax _____ E-mail _____
Real Estate Broker (Listing Firm) _____ DRE Lic. # _____
By _____ DRE Lic. # _____ Date _____
Address _____ City _____ State _____ Zip _____
Telephone _____ Fax _____ E-mail _____

ESCROW HOLDER ACKNOWLEDGMENT:
Escrow Holder acknowledges receipt of a Copy of this Agreement, (if checked, ☐ a deposit in the amount of $ _____), counter offer numbered _____, ☐ Seller's Statement of Information and ☐ Other _____ _____, and agrees to act as Escrow Holder subject to paragraph 24 of this Agreement, any supplemental escrow instructions and the terms of Escrow Holder's general provisions if any.

Escrow Holder is advised that the date of Confirmation of Acceptance of the Agreement as between Buyer and Seller is _____.

Escrow Holder _____ Escrow # _____
By _____ Date _____
Address _____
Phone/Fax/E-mail_____
Escrow Holder is licensed by the California Department of ☐ Corporations, ☐ Insurance, ☐ Real Estate. License # _____

PRESENTATION OF OFFER: (_____) Listing Broker presented this offer to Seller on _____(date).
Broker or Designee Initials

REJECTION OF OFFER: (_____)(_____) No counter offer is being made. This offer was rejected by Seller on_____(date).
Seller's Initials

THIS FORM HAS BEEN APPROVED BY THE CALIFORNIA ASSOCIATION OF REALTORS® (C.A.R.). NO REPRESENTATION IS MADE AS TO THE LEGAL VALIDITY OR ADEQUACY OF ANY PROVISION IN ANY SPECIFIC TRANSACTION. A REAL ESTATE BROKER IS THE PERSON QUALIFIED TO ADVISE ON REAL ESTATE TRANSACTIONS. IF YOU DESIRE LEGAL OR TAX ADVICE, CONSULT AN APPROPRIATE PROFESSIONAL.

This form is available for use by the entire real estate industry. It is not intended to identify the user as a REALTOR®. REALTOR® is a registered collective membership mark which may be used only by members of the NATIONAL ASSOCIATION OF REALTORS® who subscribe to its Code of Ethics.

| R E B S | I N C | Published and Distributed by:
REAL ESTATE BUSINESS SERVICES, INC.
a subsidiary of the CALIFORNIA ASSOCIATION OF REALTORS®
525 South Virgil Avenue, Los Angeles, California 90020 | Reviewed by _____
Broker or Designee _____ Date _____ |

REVISION DATE 4/10

CALIFORNIA RESIDENTIAL PURCHASE AGREEMENT (RPA-CA PAGE 8 OF 8)

 **CALIFORNIA ASSOCIATION OF REALTORS®**

REAL ESTATE TRANSFER DISCLOSURE STATEMENT
(CALIFORNIA CIVIL CODE §1102, ET SEQ.)
(C.A.R. Form TDS, Revised 10/03)

THIS DISCLOSURE STATEMENT CONCERNS THE REAL PROPERTY SITUATED IN THE CITY OF _____ _____, COUNTY OF _____, STATE OF CALIFORNIA, DESCRIBED AS _____.
THIS STATEMENT IS A DISCLOSURE OF THE CONDITION OF THE ABOVE DESCRIBED PROPERTY IN COMPLIANCE WITH SECTION 1102 OF THE CIVIL CODE AS OF (date) _____. IT IS NOT A WARRANTY OF ANY KIND BY THE SELLER(S) OR ANY AGENT(S) REPRESENTING ANY PRINCIPAL(S) IN THIS TRANSACTION, AND IS NOT A SUBSTITUTE FOR ANY INSPECTIONS OR WARRANTIES THE PRINCIPAL(S) MAY WISH TO OBTAIN.

I. COORDINATION WITH OTHER DISCLOSURE FORMS

This Real Estate Transfer Disclosure Statement is made pursuant to Section 1102 of the Civil Code. Other statutes require disclosures, depending upon the details of the particular real estate transaction (for example: special study zone and purchase-money liens on residential property).

Substituted Disclosures: The following disclosures and other disclosures required by law, including the Natural Hazard Disclosure Report/Statement that may include airport annoyances, earthquake, fire, flood, or special assessment information, have or will be made in connection with this real estate transfer, and are intended to satisfy the disclosure obligations on this form, where the subject matter is the same:

☐ Inspection reports completed pursuant to the contract of sale or receipt for deposit.
☐ Additional inspection reports or disclosures: _____
_____

II. SELLER'S INFORMATION

The Seller discloses the following information with the knowledge that even though this is not a warranty, prospective Buyers may rely on this information in deciding whether and on what terms to purchase the subject property. Seller hereby authorizes any agent(s) representing any principal(s) in this transaction to provide a copy of this statement to any person or entity in connection with any actual or anticipated sale of the property.

THE FOLLOWING ARE REPRESENTATIONS MADE BY THE SELLER(S) AND ARE NOT THE REPRESENTATIONS OF THE AGENT(S), IF ANY. THIS INFORMATION IS A DISCLOSURE AND IS NOT INTENDED TO BE PART OF ANY CONTRACT BETWEEN THE BUYER AND SELLER.

Seller ☐ is ☐ is not occupying the property.

A. The subject property has the items checked below (read across):

☐ Range	☐ Oven	☐ Microwave
☐ Dishwasher	☐ Trash Compactor	☐ Garbage Disposal
☐ Washer/Dryer Hookups		☐ Rain Gutters
☐ Burglar Alarms	☐ Smoke Detector(s)	☐ Fire Alarm
☐ TV Antenna	☐ Satellite Dish	☐ Intercom
☐ Central Heating	☐ Central Air Conditioning	☐ Evaporator Cooler(s)
☐ Wall/Window Air Conditioning	☐ Sprinklers	☐ Public Sewer System
☐ Septic Tank	☐ Sump Pump	☐ Water Softener
☐ Patio/Decking	☐ Built-in Barbecue	☐ Gazebo
☐ Sauna		
☐ Hot Tub	☐ Pool	☐ Spa
☐ Locking Safety Cover*	☐ Child Resistant Barrier*	☐ Locking Safety Cover*
☐ Security Gate(s)	☐ Automatic Garage Door Opener(s)*	☐ Number Remote Controls ____
Garage: ☐ Attached	☐ Not Attached	☐ Carport
Pool/Spa Heater: ☐ Gas	☐ Solar	☐ Electric
Water Heater: ☐ Gas	☐ Water Heater Anchored, Braced, or Strapped*	
Water Supply: ☐ City	☐ Well	☐ Private Utility or
Gas Supply: ☐ Utility	☐ Bottled	Other _____
☐ Window Screens	☐ Window Security Bars ☐ Quick Release Mechanism on Bedroom Windows*	

Exhaust Fan(s) in _____ 220 Volt Wiring in _____ Fireplace(s) in _____
☐ Gas Starter _____ ☐ Roof(s): Type: _____ Age: _____ (approx.)
☐ Other: _____
Are there, to the best of your (Seller's) knowledge, any of the above that are not in operating condition? ☐ Yes ☐ No. If yes, then describe. (Attach additional sheets if necessary): _____
_____

(*see footnote on page 2)

TDS REVISED 10/03 (PAGE 1 OF 3) Print Date

Buyer's Initials (_____)(_____)
Seller's Initials (_____)(_____)

Reviewed by _____ Date _____

EQUAL HOUSING OPPORTUNITY

REAL ESTATE TRANSFER DISCLOSURE STATEMENT (TDS PAGE 1 OF 3)

Property Address: _____ Date: _____

B. Are you (Seller) aware of any significant defects/malfunctions in any of the following? ☐ Yes ☐ No. If yes, check appropriate space(s) below.

☐ Interior Walls ☐ Ceilings ☐ Floors ☐ Exterior Walls ☐ Insulation ☐ Roof(s) ☐ Windows ☐ Doors ☐ Foundation ☐ Slab(s)
☐ Driveways ☐ Sidewalks ☐ Walls/Fences ☐ Electrical Systems ☐ Plumbing/Sewers/Septics ☐ Other Structural Components

(Describe: _____
_____
_____
_____)

If any of the above is checked, explain. (Attach additional sheets if necessary.): _____
_____
_____
_____
_____

*This garage door opener or child resistant pool barrier may not be in compliance with the safety standards relating to automatic reversing devices as set forth in Chapter 12.5 (commencing with Section 19890) of Part 3 of Division 13 of, or with the pool safety standards of Article 2.5 (commencing with Section 115920) of Chapter 5 of Part 10 of Division 104 of, the Health and Safety Code. The water heater may not be anchored, braced, or strapped in accordance with Section 19211 of the Health and Safety Code. Window security bars may not have quick release mechanisms in compliance with the 1995 edition of the California Building Standards Code.

C. Are you (Seller) aware of any of the following:

1. Substances, materials, or products which may be an environmental hazard such as, but not limited to, asbestos, formaldehyde, radon gas, lead-based paint, mold, fuel or chemical storage tanks, and contaminated soil or water on the subject property . . . . ☐ Yes ☐ No
2. Features of the property shared in common with adjoining landowners, such as walls, fences, and driveways, whose use or responsibility for maintenance may have an effect on the subject property . . . . ☐ Yes ☐ No
3. Any encroachments, easements or similar matters that may affect your interest in the subject property . . . . ☐ Yes ☐ No
4. Room additions, structural modifications, or other alterations or repairs made without necessary permits . . . . ☐ Yes ☐ No
5. Room additions, structural modifications, or other alterations or repairs not in compliance with building codes . . . . ☐ Yes ☐ No
6. Fill (compacted or otherwise) on the property or any portion thereof . . . . ☐ Yes ☐ No
7. Any settling from any cause, or slippage, sliding, or other soil problems . . . . ☐ Yes ☐ No
8. Flooding, drainage or grading problems . . . . ☐ Yes ☐ No
9. Major damage to the property or any of the structures from fire, earthquake, floods, or landslides . . . . ☐ Yes ☐ No
10. Any zoning violations, nonconforming uses, violations of "setback" requirements . . . . ☐ Yes ☐ No
11. Neighborhood noise problems or other nuisances . . . . ☐ Yes ☐ No
12. CC&R's or other deed restrictions or obligations . . . . ☐ Yes ☐ No
13. Homeowners' Association which has any authority over the subject property . . . . ☐ Yes ☐ No
14. Any "common area" (facilities such as pools, tennis courts, walkways, or other areas co-owned in undivided interest with others) . . . . ☐ Yes ☐ No
15. Any notices of abatement or citations against the property . . . . ☐ Yes ☐ No
16. Any lawsuits by or against the Seller threatening to or affecting this real property, including any lawsuits alleging a defect or deficiency in this real property or "common areas" (facilities such as pools, tennis courts, walkways, or other areas co-owned in undivided interest with others) . . . . ☐ Yes ☐ No

If the answer to any of these is yes, explain. (Attach additional sheets if necessary.): _____
_____
_____
_____
_____

Seller certifies that the information herein is true and correct to the best of the Seller's knowledge as of the date signed by the Seller.

Seller_____ Date _____

Seller_____ Date _____

Buyer's Initials (_____)(_____)
Seller's Initials (_____)(_____)

TDS REVISED 10/03 (PAGE 2 OF 3)

Reviewed by _____ Date _____

REAL ESTATE TRANSFER DISCLOSURE STATEMENT (TDS PAGE 2 OF 3)

Property Address: _____ Date: _____

III. AGENT'S INSPECTION DISCLOSURE
(To be completed only if the Seller is represented by an agent in this transaction.)

THE UNDERSIGNED, BASED ON THE ABOVE INQUIRY OF THE SELLER(S) AS TO THE CONDITION OF THE PROPERTY AND BASED ON A REASONABLY COMPETENT AND DILIGENT VISUAL INSPECTION OF THE ACCESSIBLE AREAS OF THE PROPERTY IN CONJUNCTION WITH THAT INQUIRY, STATES THE FOLLOWING:

☐ Agent notes no items for disclosure.

☐ Agent notes the following items: _____
_____
_____
_____
_____

Agent (Broker Representing Seller) _____ By _____ Date _____
          (Please Print)   (Associate Licensee or Broker Signature)

IV. AGENT'S INSPECTION DISCLOSURE
(To be completed only if the agent who has obtained the offer is other than the agent above.)

THE UNDERSIGNED, BASED ON A REASONABLY COMPETENT AND DILIGENT VISUAL INSPECTION OF THE ACCESSIBLE AREAS OF THE PROPERTY, STATES THE FOLLOWING:

☐ Agent notes no items for disclosure.

☐ Agent notes the following items: _____
_____
_____
_____
_____

Agent (Broker Obtaining the Offer) _____ By _____ Date _____
          (Please Print)   (Associate Licensee or Broker Signature)

V. BUYER(S) AND SELLER(S) MAY WISH TO OBTAIN PROFESSIONAL ADVICE AND/OR INSPECTIONS OF THE PROPERTY AND TO PROVIDE FOR APPROPRIATE PROVISIONS IN A CONTRACT BETWEEN BUYER AND SELLER(S) WITH RESPECT TO ANY ADVICE/INSPECTIONS/DEFECTS.

I/WE ACKNOWLEDGE RECEIPT OF A COPY OF THIS STATEMENT.

Seller _____ Date _____ Buyer _____ Date _____

Seller _____ Date _____ Buyer _____ Date _____

Agent (Broker Representing Seller) _____ By _____ Date _____
          (Please Print)   (Associate Licensee or Broker Signature)

Agent (Broker Obtaining the Offer) _____ By _____ Date _____
          (Please Print)   (Associate Licensee or Broker Signature)

SECTION 1102.3 OF THE CIVIL CODE PROVIDES A BUYER WITH THE RIGHT TO RESCIND A PURCHASE CONTRACT FOR AT LEAST THREE DAYS AFTER THE DELIVERY OF THIS DISCLOSURE IF DELIVERY OCCURS AFTER THE SIGNING OF AN OFFER TO PURCHASE. IF YOU WISH TO RESCIND THE CONTRACT, YOU MUST ACT WITHIN THE PRESCRIBED PERIOD.

A REAL ESTATE BROKER IS QUALIFIED TO ADVISE ON REAL ESTATE. IF YOU DESIRE LEGAL ADVICE, CONSULT YOUR ATTORNEY.

SURE TRAC
The System for Success®

Published and Distributed by:
REAL ESTATE BUSINESS SERVICES, INC.
a subsidiary of the California Association of REALTORS®
525 South Virgil Avenue, Los Angeles, California 90020

Reviewed by _____ Date _____

EQUAL HOUSING OPPORTUNITY

TDS REVISED 10/03 (PAGE 3 OF 3)

REAL ESTATE TRANSFER DISCLOSURE STATEMENT (TDS PAGE 3 OF 3)

CALIFORNIA
ASSOCIATION
OF REALTORS®

DISCLOSURE REGARDING
REAL ESTATE AGENCY RELATIONSHIP
(As required by the Civil Code)
(C.A.R. Form AD, Revised 4/06)

When you enter into a discussion with a real estate agent regarding a real estate transaction, you should from the outset understand what type of agency relationship or representation you wish to have with the agent in the transaction.

SELLER'S AGENT

A Seller's agent under a listing agreement with the Seller acts as the agent for the Seller only. A Seller's agent or a subagent of that agent has the following affirmative obligations:
To the Seller:
A Fiduciary duty of utmost care, integrity, honesty and loyalty in dealings with the Seller.
To the Buyer and the Seller:
(a) Diligent exercise of reasonable skill and care in performance of the agent's duties.
(b) A duty of honest and fair dealing and good faith.
(c) A duty to disclose all facts known to the agent materially affecting the value or desirability of the property that are not known to, or within the diligent attention and observation of, the parties.
An agent is not obligated to reveal to either party any confidential information obtained from the other party that does not involve the affirmative duties set forth above.

BUYER'S AGENT

A selling agent can, with a Buyer's consent, agree to act as agent for the Buyer only. In these situations, the agent is not the Seller's agent, even if by agreement the agent may receive compensation for services rendered, either in full or in part from the Seller. An agent acting only for a Buyer has the following affirmative obligations:
To the Buyer:
A fiduciary duty of utmost care, integrity, honesty and loyalty in dealings with the Buyer.
To the Buyer and the Seller:
(a) Diligent exercise of reasonable skill and care in performance of the agent's duties.
(b) A duty of honest and fair dealing and good faith.
(c) A duty to disclose all facts known to the agent materially affecting the value or desirability of the property that are not known to, or within the diligent attention and observation of, the parties.
An agent is not obligated to reveal to either party any confidential information obtained from the other party that does not involve the affirmative duties set forth above.

AGENT REPRESENTING BOTH SELLER AND BUYER

A real estate agent, either acting directly or through one or more associate licensees, can legally be the agent of both the Seller and the Buyer in a transaction, but only with the knowledge and consent of both the Seller and the Buyer.
In a dual agency situation, the agent has the following affirmative obligations to both the Seller and the Buyer:
(a) A fiduciary duty of utmost care, integrity, honesty and loyalty in the dealings with either the Seller or the Buyer.
(b) Other duties to the Seller and the Buyer as stated above in their respective sections.
In representing both Seller and Buyer, the agent may not, without the express permission of the respective party, disclose to the other party that the Seller will accept a price less than the listing price or that the Buyer will pay a price greater than the price offered.
The above duties of the agent in a real estate transaction do not relieve a Seller or Buyer from the responsibility to protect his or her own interests. You should carefully read all agreements to assure that they adequately express your understanding of the transaction. A real estate agent is a person qualified to advise about real estate. If legal or tax advice is desired, consult a competent professional.
Throughout your real property transaction you may receive more than one disclosure form, depending upon the number of agents assisting in the transaction. The law requires each agent with whom you have more than a casual relationship to present you with this disclosure form. You should read its contents each time it is presented to you, considering the relationship between you and the real estate agent in your specific transaction.
This disclosure form includes the provisions of Sections 2079.13 to 2079.24, inclusive, of the Civil Code set forth on page 2. Read it carefully.
I/WE ACKNOWLEDGE RECEIPT OF A COPY OF THIS DISCLOSURE AND THE PORTIONS OF THE CIVIL CODE PRINTED ON THE BACK (OR A SEPARATE PAGE).

Buyer/Seller/Landlord/Tenant_____ Date _____

Buyer/Seller/Landlord/Tenant_____ Date _____

Agent _____ DRE Lic. # _____
　　　　　　　　　　　　　　　　Real Estate Broker (Firm)
By _____ DRE Lic. # _____ Date _____
　　　　(Salesperson or Broker-Associate)

THIS FORM SHALL BE PROVIDED AND ACKNOWLEDGED AS FOLLOWS (Civil Code § 2079.14):
• When the listing brokerage company also represents Buyer, the Listing Agent shall have one AD form signed by Seller and one signed by Buyer.
• When Buyer and Seller are represented by different brokerage companies, the Listing Agent shall have one AD form signed by Seller and the Buyer's Agent shall have one AD form signed by Buyer and one signed by Seller.

R E B S
I N C

Published and Distributed by:
REAL ESTATE BUSINESS SERVICES, INC.
a subsidiary of the California Association of REALTORS®
525 South Virgil Avenue, Los Angeles, California 90020

Reviewed by _____ Date _____

EQUAL HOUSING
OPPORTUNITY

AD REVISED 4/06 (PAGE 1 OF 2) PRINT DATE

DISCLOSURE REGARDING REAL ESTATE AGENCY RELATIONSHIP (AD PAGE 1 OF 2)

CIVIL CODE SECTIONS 2079.13 THROUGH 2079.24 (2079.16 APPEARS ON THE FRONT)

2079.13 As used in Sections 2079.14 to 2079.24, inclusive, the following terms have the following meanings:
(a) "Agent" means a person acting under provisions of title 9 (commencing with Section 2295) in a real property transaction, and includes a person who is licensed as a real estate broker under Chapter 3 (commencing with Section 10130) of Part 1 of Division 4 of the Business and Professions Code, and under whose license a listing is executed or an offer to purchase is obtained. **(b)** "Associate licensee" means a person who is licensed as a real estate broker or salesperson under Chapter 3 (commencing with Section 10130) of Part 1 of Division 4 of the Business and Professions Code and who is either licensed under a broker or has entered into a written contract with a broker to act as the broker's agent in connection with acts requiring a real estate license and to function under the broker's supervision in the capacity of an associate licensee. The agent in the real property transaction bears responsibility for his or her associate licensees who perform as agents of the agent. When an associate licensee owes a duty to any principal, or to any buyer or seller who is not a principal, in a real property transaction, that duty is equivalent to the duty owed to that party by the broker for whom the associate licensee functions. **(c)** "Buyer" means a transferee in a real property transaction, and includes a person who executes an offer to purchase real property from a seller through an agent, or who seeks the services of an agent in more than a casual, transitory, or preliminary manner, with the object of entering into a real property transaction. "Buyer" includes vendee or lessee. **(d)** "Dual agent" means an agent acting, either directly or through an associate licensee, as agent for both the seller and the buyer in a real property transaction. **(e)** "Listing agreement" means a contract between an owner of real property and an agent, by which the agent has been authorized to sell the real property or to find or obtain a buyer. **(f)** "Listing agent" means a person who has obtained a listing of real property to act as an agent for compensation. **(g)** "Listing price" is the amount expressed in dollars specified in the listing for which the seller is willing to sell the real property through the listing agent. **(h)** "Offering price" is the amount expressed in dollars specified in an offer to purchase for which the buyer is willing to buy the real property. **(i)** "Offer to purchase" means a written contract executed by a buyer acting through a selling agent which becomes the contract for the sale of the real property upon acceptance by the seller. **(j)** "Real property" means any estate specified by subdivision (1) or (2) of Section 761 in property which constitutes or is improved with one to four dwelling units, any leasehold in this type of property exceeding one year's duration, and mobile homes, when offered for sale or sold through an agent pursuant to the authority contained in Section 10131.6 of the Business and Professions Code. **(k)** "Real property transaction" means a transaction for the sale of real property in which an agent is employed by one or more of the principals to act in that transaction, and includes a listing or an offer to purchase. **(l)** "Sell," "sale," or "sold" refers to a transaction for the transfer of real property from the seller to the buyer, and includes exchanges of real property between the seller and buyer, transactions for the creation of a real property sales contract within the meaning of Section 2985, and transactions for the creation of a leasehold exceeding one year's duration. **(m)** "Seller" means the transferor in a real property transaction, and includes an owner who lists real property with an agent, whether or not a transfer results, or who receives an offer to purchase real property of which he or she is the owner from an agent on behalf of another. "Seller" includes both a vendor and a lessor. **(n)** "Selling agent" means a listing agent who acts alone, or an agent who acts in cooperation with a listing agent, and who sells or finds and obtains a buyer for the real property, or an agent who locates property for a buyer or who finds a buyer for a property for which no listing exists and presents an offer to purchase to the seller. **(o)** "Subagent" means a person to whom an agent delegates agency powers as provided in Article 5 (commencing with Section 2349) of Chapter 1 of Title 9. However, "subagent" does not include an associate licensee who is acting under the supervision of an agent in a real property transaction.

2079.14 Listing agents and selling agents shall provide the seller and buyer in a real property transaction with a copy of the disclosure form specified in Section 2079.16, and, except as provided in subdivision (c), shall obtain a signed acknowledgement of receipt from that seller or buyer, except as provided in this section or Section 2079.15, as follows: **(a)** The listing agent, if any, shall provide the disclosure form to the seller prior to entering into the listing agreement. **(b)** The selling agent shall provide the disclosure form to the seller as soon as practicable prior to presenting the seller with an offer to purchase, unless the selling agent previously provided the seller with a copy of the disclosure form pursuant to subdivision (a). **(c)** Where the selling agent does not deal on a face-to-face basis with the seller, the disclosure form prepared by the selling agent may be furnished to the seller (and acknowledgement of receipt obtained for the selling agent from the seller) by the listing agent, or the selling agent may deliver the disclosure form by certified mail addressed to the seller at his or her last known address, in which case no signed acknowledgement of receipt is required. **(d)** The selling agent shall provide the disclosure form to the buyer as soon as practicable prior to execution of the buyer's offer to purchase, except that if the offer to purchase is not prepared by the selling agent, the selling agent shall present the disclosure form to the buyer not later than the next business day after the selling agent receives the offer to purchase from the buyer.

2079.15 In any circumstance in which the seller or buyer refuses to sign an acknowledgement of receipt pursuant to Section 2079.14, the agent, or an associate licensee acting for an agent, shall set forth, sign, and date a written declaration of the facts of the refusal.

2079.17 (a) As soon as practicable, the selling agent shall disclose to the buyer and seller whether the selling agent is acting in the real property transaction exclusively as the buyer's agent, exclusively as the seller's agent, or as a dual agent representing both the buyer and the seller. This relationship shall be confirmed in the contract to purchase and sell real property or in a separate writing executed or acknowledged by the seller, the buyer, and the selling agent prior to or coincident with execution of that contract by the buyer and the seller, respectively. **(b)** As soon as practicable, the listing agent shall disclose to the seller whether the listing agent is acting in the real property transaction exclusively as the seller's agent, or as a dual agent representing both the buyer and seller. This relationship shall be confirmed in the contract to purchase and sell real property or in a separate writing executed or acknowledged by the seller and the listing agent prior to or coincident with the execution of that contract by the seller.
(c) The confirmation required by subdivisions (a) and (b) shall be in the following form.

_____ **(DO NOT COMPLETE. SAMPLE ONLY)** _____ is the agent of (check one): ☐ the seller exclusively; or ☐ both the buyer and seller.
(Name of Listing Agent)

_____ **(DO NOT COMPLETE. SAMPLE ONLY)** _____ is the agent of (check one): ☐ the buyer exclusively; or ☐ the seller exclusively; or
(Name of Selling Agent if not the same as the Listing Agent)   ☐ both the buyer and seller.

(d) The disclosures and confirmation required by this section shall be in addition to the disclosure required by Section 2079.14.

2079.18 No selling agent in a real property transaction may act as an agent for the buyer only, when the selling agent is also acting as the listing agent in the transaction.

2079.19 The payment of compensation or the obligation to pay compensation to an agent by the seller or buyer is not necessarily determinative of a particular agency relationship between an agent and the seller or buyer. A listing agent and a selling agent may agree to share any compensation or commission paid, or any right to any compensation or commission for which an obligation arises as the result of a real estate transaction, and the terms of any such agreement shall not necessarily be determinative of a particular relationship.

2079.20 Nothing in this article prevents an agent from selecting, as a condition of the agent's employment, a specific form of agency relationship not specifically prohibited by this article if the requirements of Section 2079.14 and Section 2079.17 are complied with.

2079.21 A dual agent shall not disclose to the buyer that the seller is willing to sell the property at a price less than the listing price, without the express written consent of the seller. A dual agent shall not disclose to the seller that the buyer is willing to pay a price greater than the offering price, without the express written consent of the buyer. This section does not alter in any way the duty or responsibility of a dual agent to any principal with respect to confidential information other than price.

2079.22 Nothing in this article precludes a listing agent from also being a selling agent, and the combination of these functions in one agent does not, of itself, make that agent a dual agent.

2079.23 A contract between the principal and agent may be modified or altered to change the agency relationship at any time before the performance of the act which is the object of the agency with the written consent of the parties to the agency relationship.

2079.24 Nothing in this article shall be construed to either diminish the duty of disclosure owed buyers and sellers by agents and their associate licensees, subagents, and employees or to relieve agents and their associate licensees, subagents, and employees from liability for their conduct in connection with acts governed by this article or for any breach of a fiduciary duty or a duty of disclosure.

Seller's/Landlord's Initials (_____)(_____)
Buyer's/Tenant's Initials   (_____)(_____)

AD REVISED 4/06 (PAGE 2 OF 2)

Reviewed by _____ Date _____

EQUAL HOUSING OPPORTUNITY

DISCLOSURE REGARDING REAL ESTATE AGENCY RELATIONSHIPS (AD PAGE 2 OF 2)

Student Learning Outcomes for Module 4

Beyond

At the completion of this module, students will be able to:

✔ Calculate the amount they should be saving every month for maintenance.

✔ Report what an agent should continue to do after home purchase.

✔ List two ways to get involved with the community.

Index

About the Author

Chris Sorensen is executive director of the Homeownership Education Learning Program (H.E.L.P.), a nonprofit corporation that provides assistance to homeowners struggling to buy or maintain a home in troubled economic times. Chris Sorensen has been in real estate and banking for more than 20 years. He is a former city council member and mayor. As founder and creator of H.E.L.P., he hopes to give back to his community and raise the ethics bar for the housing industry.

Contact Chris Sorensen via email at Chris@theSorensenTeam.com

About the California Community College Real Estate Education Center

In 1975, California's real estate industry and its community colleges were all in accord when the state legislature established an endowment to support real estate education in the state's 106 community colleges. The California Department of Real Estate established the endowment by donating $1.9 million to the California Community Colleges from its Education, Research and Recovery Fund, which is funded through license fees. The fund has since grown to $3.5 million thanks to a generous donation by the Department of Real Estate in 2010.

The original endowment fund agreement, signed by the Real Estate Commissioner and the Community College Chancellor states that the fund's objective is to "advance the professionalization of the field through real estate courses in the California Community Colleges." The fund assures perpetual financial support for the enhancement of real estate education because only the interest earned may be spent to achieve the program's goals. The clear mandate from the legislature was for interest income generated by the fund to be used to develop and improve programs. These funds were to supplement not supplant college support for real estate programs.

The initial $1.9 million donation is divided into two parts: one for student scholarships and the for educational program enhancement. The scholarship program, which is intended for worthy and disadvantaged students, is administered by the California Community Colleges Chancellor's Office in Sacramento. To date, more than $825,000 has been awarded to some 800 real estate career-minded students throughout the state. The educational enhancement part of the endowment has been administered by the Real Estate Education Center founded in Modesto at the Yosemite Community College District and currently housed at the City College of San Francisco Community College District.

The Real Estate Education Center pursues several activities throughout the year to meet its goal of enhancing real estate education in the over 100 community colleges in California. Over 75 of these colleges offer real estate education programs that perform some or all of the following services:

- Sponsors three real estate educator conferences each year in San Diego, Los Angeles, and Northern California regional locations

- Publishes instructor and student study guides in the major real estate pre-licensing course areas

- Coordinates endowment advisory board committee activity

- Maintains a link with government, trade, industry professional organizations, and other educational institutions that have an interest in real estate education

- Monitors enrollment trends

- Acts as a clearinghouse for community college real estate education information

Most recently, the Real Estate Education Center partnered with the Department of Real Estate's Financial Literacy Initiative to conduct an outreach program in California's community colleges. The current economic times underscore the need for financially literate homeowners armed with the decision-making tools necessary for successful homeownership. To this end, a series of four live seminars entitled, "Financial Sense to White Picket Fence," were conducted between June and November 2010 in Northern, Central, Southern and Inland Empire California community colleges. The four seminar segments, "Budgeting, Borrowing, Buying and Beyond," were also offered weekly in August as webinars. As part of this program, 3C Media Solutions, the educational media distribution network of the California Community Colleges, broadcast live streaming video of the October seminar at El Camino College, Torrance. This student companion guide reflects the California Community College Real Estate Education Center's contribution to financial literacy education for all Californians. This guide is suitable for secondary school, college, and adult educational programs. Use it to complement in-classroom instruction or as a valuable self-study tool.

More information about the Real Estate Education Center and its activities can be found at http://ccsf.edu/real_estate_education_center or by emailing the center directly at reec@ccsf.edu. The center's mailing address is: Real Estate Education Center, San Francisco City College—Downtown Campus, 88 Fourth Street, Room 324, San Francisco, CA 94103. The telephone number is (415) 267-6550 and facsimile is (415) 267-6518.

Colophon

Design This book was designed for the California Community College Real Estate Education Center, based at the City College of San Francisco, by Leigh McLellan Design in San Francisco, http://www.leighmcdesign.com

Typefaces ITC Giovanni is used for the text and ITC Giovanni and Frutiger for display, composed by Leigh McLellan Design in Adobe Indesign CS4

Color digital printing and binding by Lightning Source Inc., La Vergne, Tennessee. Lightning Source Inc. processes are certified by the following green certification organizations: The Forest Stewardship Council® and the Sustainable Forestry Initiative®

Images in the Ask the Expert boxes are from *Bizarro*, used by permission of Dan Piraro. Visit him at http://bizarrocomic.blogspot.com

Financial Literacy Team from left to right: Leo Bello, City College of San Francisco; Mark Castillo, Grouchy Tiger Productions; Shannon Faulk, moral support; Dionne Faulk, DRE; Carol Jensen, CCCREEC; Christine Chappell, H.E.L.P; Steven Green, Presidio Technical Services; Mary Jane Green, Presidio Administrative Services; Chris Sorensen, H.E.L.P; Jorna Tolosa, Grouchy Tiger Productions; John Black, San Jose City College; Kim Romena, Photography

Not in this picture but indispensible: Robin Pugh, City College of San Francisco; Leigh McLellan, Leigh McLellan Design; Margaret Light, Photography; Ivan Navarro, volunteer extraordinaire

CPSIA information can be obtained
at www.ICGtesting.com
Printed in the USA
LVIC04n0139090116
469881LV00002B/2